# The Juxtaposition Of Organisms

By Narcis Marincat

©2015 Narcis Marincat, All Rights Reserved

# Introduction

After an interesting journey filled with unexpected events, an adventurer finds, at last, a palace filled with treasure. There are jewels of all kinds, there is gold, and silver, and sapphire, there is fine cloth, there are instruments of shapes and sizes the likes of which he has never seen. But he needs help to bring all this treasure back to his home land, and so he seeks the help of the king. He knows the king to be a busy man, and that his only chance is to bring something to the king that will draw out his attention for the brief span of time our adventurer will have when he gains an audience with the royal figure.

The adventurer has nothing with which to carry large items, and he knows his journey back home to be long, and so he looks around the palace for something, something small, something that can fit inside his pocket, something that distills the whole treasure trove he has found, that can represent it.

This book is what he finds, and you, the audience, are the king.

The book's title and subtitles are self-revealing. Simply put, this work seeks to juxtapose human society with the human body by tracing the outlines of a language applicable to the inner workings of both, and discusses consciousness, morality, and biology from that perspective. It was penned as a response to the claim that my first book, In Principio Res, was written in a much too complicated form, and that although the ideas written within it are "very interesting", they have been much better understood through the conversations I've had with various people on the subject.

The book is composed of two parts. The first part discusses the main ideas laid down within In Principio Res in an easygoing, conversational tone, so as to convey them as clearly as possible. Even though it sometimes makes reference to In Principio Res, this part of the book is really self-contained, so there's no need to study In Principio Res to understand the concepts discussed herein. The references made to In Principio Res are really just a prop tool for the conversational tone used, and it also betrays the various discussion I've had about the book as its source of inspiration. The second part is comprised of a series of papers with revealing titles, written to go at the core of each major topic addressed. The two parts of this book are meant to be complementary. That is, some of the things spoken about in the first part may not be in the second part, and vice versa.

Notably, references are provided in the papers contained by the second part of the book, so that the first part can be read as simple prose, without the burden of having to stop and dissect the proof for the claims made.

You decide if the book shines brightly enough to warrant a return to the castle.

# Part 1: Explanation

## Chapter I. Cells

In Principio Res starts out with the idea that cells are very complex entities. For a long time, it was considered that cells were simple beings, like molecular factories operating on predictable rules. But with the improvement of microscopes, imaging techniques used, and ways of recording cellular activity, cells have been increasingly presenting themselves as highly intricate entities, capable of unique actions that are oftentimes quite unpredictable.

The book places an emphasis on nervous cells, which have a particularly interesting history. Brain tissue is notoriously hard to analyze because it is very sensitive, so for a long time - up until the last decade of the 19$^{th}$ century - you couldn't really analyze the microscopic structure of a brain without damaging it. That's how it could be generally considered up until that time that unlike the rest of the tissue within the body, which was already known to be made of discrete cells, the brain was actually a continuous network that was fused together - there were no independent cells in it. That changed when new staining techniques were introduced in the 1890's which allowed people to analyze the microstructure of brain tissue without damaging it, and they could see that there were in fact tiny gaps that separated one nervous cell from another, which we now call synaptic clefts.

Still, in the beginning, there was considered to be only a handful of types of nervous cells in the brain. But as microscopes improved, that number grew and grew, until today, it is estimated that there are about 800 to 1000 different types of neurons, and it's probable that as imaging devices get better and better at recording cellular activity in the live brain, that number will continue to expand.

Also, for the better part of the 20th century, it was considered that the connections between neurons - the synapses - become largely fixed during adolescence, and it's mainly the thickness of those connections that change with learning. But with the introduction of new types of microscopes at the beginning of the 1990's, like 2-photon microscopy, scientists could begin to record the activity of single nervous cells within the live brain in certain conditions, and what they have found in the past two decades is that in fact nervous cells are very dynamic, in that they may form new connections between them, terminate old ones, that they communicate in various ways, that they pass chemical messengers between them not only at synapses, and the reason for choosing which chemical messengers that they do pass are highly complex, and so on. So basically, they discovered that nervous cells, rather than being these mechanical things, are in fact, unique, independent, unpredictable entities - and really, the book talks about how this is true of all types of cells, not just nervous cells, to which some of these imaging techniques apply as well and which have been shown to be quite unique.

Then, the book discusses the difference in size and speed between humans and cells. It says that if cells are small and move very fast from our perspective - for example a typical nervous cell sends upwards of 100 nervous impulses to its neighbors every second - so if they are small and move very fast from our perspective, it doesn't mean that they are small or that they move very fast from their "perspective" - if we were to name it a "perspective". That is to say, if cells can process information, which their unique activity shows that they can, let the result of that information processing be called their individual "perspective". And from their perspective, cellular size is the normal size, and cellular action is not very fast, it's the normal speed. To make this easier to understand, a thought experiment is introduced.

   Imagine, the book says, that a group of extraterrestrials takes a trip of exploration around the galaxies, when, upon venturing close to our solar system, their spaceship dutifully picks up a strange fluorescence emanated from the surface of our planet, so they decide to take a closer look and investigate. Now, these are not your average extraterrestrial beings - they are extremely large. So large, in fact, that each one of them is comparable in size to our planet. Not only that, but imagine that with this size difference there would be a difference in their speed, such that a year from our human perspective would equal for them to the timespan of merely a day. Finally, these extraterrestrials reach the vicinity of Earth, they take their endoscope-like instruments, peer through Earth's cloudy atmosphere, and what do they see? Well, they see that an organism is growing on the surface of this planet, and rather than being "fluorescence", what their spaceship picked up was in fact a type of bioluminescence emanating by this organism. The organism that they would see would of course be human society. Here, it's important to note that these extraterrestrials would be completely different in nature from us, and that this is the first time they've seen anything like this organism in their entire history of space explorations. Ok then, put yourself in the extraterrestrials' shoes. How would they, being so large and so slow, see human society? Well, they would see it as a whole…as kind of like a slime-mold, a fungus streaked along the Earth's surface. And even though they would be looking at human society, they wouldn't be able to see humans, because humans would be of a microscopic size.

But let's say that these are science-prone lifeforms, so what they do next is use microscope-like instruments to uninvasively analyze the microscopic structure of this organism growing on the surface of Earth, and what they discover is that this organism has a fundamental structural and functional unit - the human. They conclude that this organism is made of humans, which are responsible for everything from the metabolic function of this organism, to its growth (that is, when human beings grow in number, the size of the organism grows). So, the perspective of these alien scientists in relation to human society is not unlike the perspective of human beings in relation to their fellow man. For example, you look at me, and you see me as a single entity, one organism, even though you know that my body is made up of countless cells, and when I talk or move, you see it as "me" talking or moving when it's actually the result of these cells cooperating in large numbers with one another.

At the same time, the alien scientists would have a very simplistic view of humans, based on the limited information their scientific instruments can pick up from human activity. For example, human speech is a form of communication that is unique to our order of magnitude - just think of how strange it would seem for the alien scientists that we are able to communicate by passing airwaves of various frequencies between one another. In space, there wouldn't be any air, so for them that would be an entirely novel concept. This means that their scientific instruments would probably not be equipped with a microphone that would pick up these airwaves, because they would have no concept of microphones - but even if they would be, due to the difference in speed between us and them, an entire human monologue would vanish in the flash of an instant, so they would probably interpret it as a blip…an impulse, and not see it speech for what it is. No, what they would be able to do though is make assumptions about human beings based on the big picture: For example, they may reach the conclusion that after birth, a human being picks up the general activities of those within its surroundings, because their microscopes would allow them to see that if a human was born in an area of human society in which most people can drive cars, that human would also have a high probability of driving a car. Or if a human was born in an area of human society in which most people get their food from big nourishment hubs - supermarkets - that human would also have a high probability of doing the same.

So, bottom line, due to the difference in size and speed between us and them, as well as the limitations of their scientific instruments the alien scientists would have a very simplistic view of humans, and it would just be natural for them to see human society as a whole, and interpret things as such. If for example they were to devise an experiment in which they would send an asteroid towards Earth to see what would happen, and a missile was to fly off from some part of human society and obliterate the asteroid as a result, they would interpret the sending of the missile as the action of human society, rather than the result of countless actions performed by human beings within human society - it would just be natural for them, from their perspective, to interpret things that way, just as it is natural for you to interpret my talking as my action, rather than the result of countless cells within my body cooperating with one another in order to make this speech happen.

Following this trail of logic, it's quite probable that our simplistic view of cells is largely due to the difference in size and speed between us and them, as well as the limited information our scientific instruments can pick up from the real-time activity of single cells, a theory that is supported by the fact that with each improvement in microscope design, staining technique or way of recording cells, the complexity of nervous cell activity as we see it has increased, rather than stayed the same or decreased.

# Chapter II. Consciousness

Then the book goes on to ask: What is human consciousness? Traditionally, thoughts have been described as electrochemical patterns arising from the activity of nervous cells, which doesn't tell us much about how the activity of single nervous cells is connected to consciousness. But we are now entertaining that 1. cells are independent, unpredictable, autonomous entities capable of unique actions and 2. that there is a difference in size and speed between humans and single cells that make us think cells move very fast and that their activities are rather simple, when in fact from their perspective their move at a normal pace, and can be seen to engage in quite complex activities.

So then, the book puts out the following theory: What if human consciousness is in fact made up of elements nervous cells and cellular networks synthesize that they focus upon collectively? The idea is as follows: Think about books, movies, songs within our human society. People synthesize - that's the technical term used in the book, which basically means create - so people synthesize all kinds of elements - books, movies, all kinds. Some of these elements are synthesized by one human - like a book for example, while others are synthesized by groups of humans, like movies, which usually involve a movie studio, full of people that are involved the making of a movie. And some of these elements have the necessary qualities to become very popular within human society - the technical definition within the book is to say that it attracts the collective attention of human beings. Think of a very popular book that a lot of people have read, or a very popular movie that a lot of people has seen. Now, In Principio Res puts forth the theory that by and large, the same thing happens within a person's brain, like yours or mine. That is, nervous cells and cellular networks synthesize various elements - like thoughts, images, feelings, bodily sensations - elements that are of course specific to their order of magnitude. And some of these elements have the necessary qualities to attract the collective attention of nervous cells and cellular networks - that is, to become very popular within your nervous system - and these are your conscious thoughts.

One common characteristic of all these elements is that their essence lies in the information they carry rather than the physical medium which carries them - a book for example can be written on paper, or be read on the computer, yet it's the same book - but other than that, like I said, elements which arise within your consciousness are specific to the cellular order of magnitude, while elements synthesized by humans are specific to ours.

Now for you, the time it takes for a thought to be synthesized by your cells may seem almost instant - for example, when you focus upon a problem, a solution may emerge within your consciousness moments afterwards, so there seems to be no time for individual cells to be actively engaged in the synthesis of those thoughts. But time may move much slower from the perspective of a cell. It's similar to how the synthesis of a movie by a movie studio may seem like a long time from a human perspective, but when looked at from the perspective of the alien scientists, it would be a much shorter timespan.

Alright, so what evidence is there for this theory of human consciousness - that human consciousness is comprised of elements cells and cellular networks synthesize, and for the semblance of human consciousness with the collective focus of human beings? Well, there are quite a few lines of evidence.

For example, what happens when people collectively focus upon an element some of them have synthesized - that is, when that element gains a great deal of popularity? Let's take an example: M*A*S*H. You've heard of M*A*S*H, right? First, there was a book that appeared with that title. The book wasn't very popular, but it inspired the making of the movie M*A*S*H in 1970, which went out to become a great success with 5 Oscar nominations. Because it was such a great success, the movie, which attracted the collective attention of human beings, inspired news articles, and fan art, and so on, as well as the TV-show spinoff, which in turn had the necessary qualities to attract the collective focus of human beings and which in fact became more popular than the movie.

So, a very broad analysis of what happened is that the movie M*A*S*H emerged within the collective focus of human beings, inspiring the synthesis of numerous elements by human beings found throughout human society, and from among all these related elements the TV show spinoff had in turn the necessary qualities to attract the collective attention of human beings. And this is what happens in the brain - for example, right now you are listening to my words, as I speak, which in this theory, means that your cells are focusing upon these words collectively - they are popular within your nervous system. And what happens is, as you are listening you also get various related elements within your consciousness - thoughts about what I'm saying, images that help you visualize what I'm saying, even feelings - and in this theory of consciousness, these are all elements that your cells and cellular networks synthesize that attract their collective attention as they focus collectively upon my words - that is, as you're consciously focusing upon my words. There are also elements your cells and cellular networks synthesize as you are listening to my words that do not have the necessary qualities to attract their collective focus, and these elements are part of your subconscious - just like some of the things people synthesized as a result of the movie M*A*S*H becoming very popular - like fan art, or news articles - did not have the necessary qualities to attract the collective attention of human beings, unlike the TV series.

So, broadly speaking, when human beings focused collectively on the movie M*A*S*H, numerous elements that related to it were synthesized, some of which had the necessary qualities to in turn attract the collective focus of human beings - the TV series M*A*S*H being a notable example, and a similar thing happens within your nervous system. When your cells and cellular networks focus collectively on something, like my speech, numerous elements that relate to it are synthesized, some of which have in turn the necessary qualities to attract their collective attention - like the feelings, and the visualizations, and the thoughts relating to my speech that you are consciously having right now. Then these feelings, visualizations and thoughts go through the same process, and so do the following popular elements your cells and cellular networks synthesize, and so on...and that's how the continuous stream of thoughts of your mind is born. And whatever elements are synthesized that do not attract the collective attention of your cells and cellular networks are part of your subconscious.

Another simple proof for the relationship between the collective focus of human beings and human consciousness, and thus for the validity of the theory of human consciousness proposed here is the similarity between the process by which we, the general population of humans, get to see space through observatories and telescopes, and how you consciously see the world through your eyesight. You know that what you consciously perceive as vision is not the raw footage picked up by your eyes. If you were to see images that come through the eye directly as the cells in the eye first receives them, you would have a blurry image that constantly moves around due to the eye's micromovements, with a blind spot somewhere in the upper visual field of each eye from where the optic nerve connects to the retina, as there are no retinal cells there, with color in the middle of your visual field and black and white all around for the most part, with blood vessels masking the image...In other words, it would not be the clear, full color, seamless world that you do consciously perceive. Instead, that raw footage picked up by your eyes serves merely as the inspiration for cells and cellular networks within your brain that are specialized in processing it...Cells which, inspired by that raw footage, synthesize elements that become the rich visual experience of the world that you are consciously perceiving right now.

This is not unlike how the colored, beautiful images of space that we human beings commonly pass along between us, that become popular within human society are not the actual raw footage that are captured by observatories and telescopes around the world, but the refined version of these images.

Telescopes like Hubble for example take black-and-white pictures using different filters to capture particular wavelengths of light, normally three to four. Then, an astronomer or a team of astronomers works on putting them together. They begin by assigning each grey-scale image a color – for example, select one image and make it blue, select another to make it green, and another to make it red. As a general rule, those people who specialize in this field seek to assign red to the image showing the longest wavelengths of light and blue to the one showing the shortest, in order to reflect the relationship among the colors of the visible spectrum. Following that, the pictures are overlaid on top of one another to produce a full color picture, not unlike how televisions and computer screens create color. Finally, the colored images are corrected for any errors, cropped, and orientated to give off the best effect; Videos of space are usually artist's renderings inspired by such pictures. One statement from NASA astutely summarized the process by saying that "Creating color images out of the original black-and-white exposures is equal parts art and science."

So, both in the case of us humans in general, and the general population of nervous cells and cellular networks within your body, the picture of their surroundings acquired isn't the raw footage picked up by the "sense organs" of the organism they are part of - eyes in the case of cells, observatories and telescopes in the case of human beings - but the elements synthesized by some of these basic units that are specialized in refining those images - cells and cellular networks in the visual cortex in the case of cells, astronomers and the like in the case of human beings.

So, these are just two examples of how human consciousness and the collective focus of human beings resembles, and two lines of evidence to show that we can consider human consciousness as the elements synthesized by cells and cellular networks that they focus on collectively, kind of like movies, songs, books that become very popular within human society. There are other examples too, other lines of evidence, and we might get to some of them later. But anyway, from here, the book begins to enter into the concept of morality.

# Chapter III. Morality

So, what we've learned up until now is that you, a human being, can be seen as a basic unit within human society, just like cells are basic units within your body. Also, there are a number of similarities between human consciousness and the collective focus of human beings, lending credence to the theory that human consciousness is comprised of the elements nervous cells and cellular networks synthesize which attract their collective attention (feelings, sensations, ideas, images, etc.) not unlike how human beings and human networks synthesize elements within human society, like books, movies and songs, some of which become very popular.

Now, what one consciously focuses upon is important in more ways than one, and each of us knows that intuitively. That's why, for example, if you want to solve a problem, you focus upon it, because you know that it's how you may discover a solution to it. From the perspective of the theory of consciousness introduced in this book - which, by the way, is called the together-knowing theory of consciousness - from the perspective of this theory, this particular importance of one's conscious focus is explained by pointing to the fact that whatever one focuses upon is whatever the cells and cellular networks within one's nervous systems synthesize elements around, the elements which in the next moment may attract their collective attention and thus emerge within one's consciousness. That's why, as per our example, if you want to find a solution to a problem, you focus upon it - because the cells and cellular networks of your nervous system will synthesize various elements that relate to that problem, some of which will be solutions which may attract their collective attention and thus emerge within your consciousness, leading to that problem being solved.

But does the collective focus of human beings bear equal importance within human society? To put it another way: Is what we, as human beings, focus upon collectively important? Why yes it is, in more ways than one, because things that are very popular within human society get funded - oculus rift, the new virtual reality headset that is making waves in the VR industry is a good contemporary example; things that are very popular get disseminated, like the widespread distribution of popular movies, books, songs, video games; things that are very popular get adopted, like the automobile; things that are very popular get improved upon, like the ever-improving novel designs for 3D printers that seek to make them more efficient, simpler, less expensive, etc.; things that are very popular get analyzed, scrutinized, like the unfortunate case of airplane crashes; things that are very popular become the inspiration for other elements humans synthesize, like the example of a popular movie leading to the synthesis of fan art, blog posts, documentaries, spin-offs, etc. So, what we as human beings focus upon collectively is important. But the thing is, we each contribute to what elements synthesized by humans become very popular through our individual actions, through the elements synthesized by human beings that we decide to assimilate, to talk about with our friends, family and neighbors, whether it's a book, a movie, an invention, a song, a website, a news article, an idea. We all participate in the "decision" of which elements synthesized by human beings emerge within our collective focus through the elements that we decide to synthesize and help synthesize, through the elements we decide to think about, to talk to one another about, through the elements that we decide to share with one another.

This is where I see true democracy: Each one of us actively participates towards establishing the direction in which we turn our collective attention through our own individual conscious attention and through what we choose to share with those around us, and this collective attention means development, growth for the object of focus, regardless of whether it's a human being, an invention, a theory…whatever it is.

So then, ask yourself, "What types of elements would I like for the cells of my body to help synthesize and elevate within my conscious awareness?" Whatever the answer may be, you should seek to synthesize and help elevate within the collective focus of human beings - that is, help promote - elements that bear the same qualities for human society, because you are in relation to human society what a nervous cell is in relation to your body and consciousness. This is the first moral precept put forth by the book: **Do unto the collective focus of human beings as you would have the cells of your body do unto your consciousness.** Now, your answer to the aforementioned question "What types of elements would I like for the cells of my body to help synthesize and elevate within my conscious awareness?" may be unique, but for the purpose of this conversation, let's give a general, commonsense answer, and say that the elements you would like for the cells of your body to help synthesize and elevate within your conscious awareness are those that lead to a sense of conscious awe (like a thought about the wonder of simply being alive), that provide you with happiness (like a good joke), that help you establish meaningful goals (like eating well doing enough physical exercise to stay healthy) and that help you achieve the goals in question in a way that's intelligent and empathetic towards your cells (i.e. ideas of how achieve your goals in a fun, intelligent way). And because all such elements would have at their fundament the happiness and well-being of your cells (consider that your conscious happiness is really the general happiness of your cells and cellular networks), you can say that they are elements that, in a word, help make the world you are a better place for the greatest number of your cells.

So then, you should seek to synthesize and help elevate within the collective focus of human beings elements that provide the general population of human beings with a sense of conscious awe, elements that generate happiness, elements that help establish meaningful goals for human society as a whole - that is, goals which refer to the general population of human beings and to which the general population would agree to - and elements that help achieve the goals in question in a way that's intelligent and empathetic towards all human beings. (i.e. that help achieve those goals in a way that's intelligent and fun for human beings in general)....Elements that, in a word, help make the world we are part of a better place for the greatest number of human beings. As mentioned before, these elements can be of any nature, from books to TV shows, to academic papers, to inventions....Elements that are synthesized or discovered by people around the world.

This then is the first moral precept: Do unto the collective focus of human beings as you would have the cells of your body do unto your consciousness.

The second question that you can ask yourself is "How would I like for the cells of my body to treat their neighboring cells?" Here too, whatever your answer may be, you should seek to do the same to your neighbor within human society.

This then is the second moral precept put forth by the book: **Do unto your neighbor as you would have the cells of your body do unto their neighboring cells.** Again, your answer to the question "How would I like for the cells of my body to treat their neighboring cells?" may be unique, but let's go ahead and give a general response with the assumption that you want your cells to treat one another with empathy, and whenever possible to help each other thrive, because you know that if the general population of cells within your body thrive, you thrive. Saying this may sound like you're giving your cells human qualities, but in fact it is widely known that if one cell within the body is damaged, the cells surrounding it can come to its aid, and who knows what other things unaccounted for by our scientific instruments cells can do to positively influence their neighboring cells. So then, you should seek to treat your neighbor with empathy, to help your neighbor thrive, because in the same vein, if the general population of human beings thrives, then human society will thrive.

This then is the second moral precept put forth by the book: Do unto your neighbor as you would have the cells of your body do unto their neighboring cells, and together with the first one,

Do unto the collective focus of human beings as you would have the cells of your body do unto your consciousness, forms the basic moral precepts of the book from which all other derive.

But it's important to note however that one shouldn't follow these moral guidelines due to some spiritual imperative. These are materialistic moral guidelines derived from overlapping the human being with human society, which means that one should follow them most of all because they are **logical and useful**.

We've already briefly addressed their logic, but before we can truly understand and address their utility, which includes ideas like providing human beings throughout human society with their basic necessities, we would have to first turn to another main topic of the book: Evolution.

# Chapter IV.Evolution

Let's then return to the perspective of the alien scientists, and look at human society again. We've mentioned that from their vantage point, human society would look like an organism. But what kind of organism would it be? It can't be a multicellular organism because by definition, multicellular organisms are organisms comprised of many cells. So, if we are to name organisms comprised of many cells as multicellular organisms, let us then define organisms comprised of many animals as **multizoa organisms**. The word *zoia* is the Greek word for "animals", so it can be translated as an organism comprised of many animals. So then, let us look at human society as a multizoa organism. What can be said about it?

Well, the first striking feature is that human society is a self-emergent multizoa organism, the first of its kind; It does not have any parent. This is in contrast to any multizoa organism that would arise in the future - like human colonies that would be established on other planets, or starships that would be built- because they would all trace their ancestry to human society; they would have emerged through multizoa reproduction.

So, human society, as a multizoa organism, is basically on par with the first cell to have emerged within nature - dubbed by human scientists as the protocell - as well as with the first multicellular organisms to have emerged within nature, which we may refer to as protomulticellular organisms. In other words, we may call human society a protomultizoa organism.

Now, there are many contentious points about the evolution of cellular organisms, but one thing is for certain - in order for cellular organisms to have evolved over time to the extent that they did up until now, that first cell, that protocell would have had to develop the ability to reproduce. So let's say that human society, as a protomultizoa organism, develops the ability to reproduce, which basically means that it develops the ability to establish colonies on other planets and\or to build starships that can carry human beings in large numbers, each of which would be a multizoa organism in its own right.

The question then is: Would multizoa organisms evolve generation after generation, just like multicellular organisms have, and what would drive that evolutionary process?

In order to answer this question, let's return to the perspective of the alien scientists. In Principio Res says to imagine that after they performed a number of scientific experiments on our present human society, the alien scientists eventually left this galactic area satisfied with the data they've collected. Their species did not come back to our corner of the universe for a few billion years, after which time their interest in human society suddenly rekindled. So, they decided to see what changed since their kind first ventured here, and what they discovered upon returning simply astonished them. The long-past first expedition that their ancestors went on years ago (billions of years from the perspective of human beings) documented the existence of only one multizoa organism, our human society. But now, upon returning, they were surprised to witness the existence of a large number and variety of multizoa organisms, displaying strikingly different structural differences - that is, what the alien scientists would consider multizoa traits - and behaviors between them. Some of these multizoa organisms were indeed rooted to the surface of planets and somewhat resembled the description of our human society, whereas others had motile, agile bodies and engaged in complex activities - what we would consider to be human-built starships. With the help of their advanced scientific instruments, the alien scientists discovered stationary as well as motile multizoa organisms that lived underwater on various planets as well. In other words, in contrast to the first expedition, what they now found was an incredible display of multizoa life, with multizoa organisms of various shapes and sizes, adapted to various environments.

Now, they may very well wonder how the number of multizoa organisms increased so: Whether multizoa organisms emerge through spontaneous generation, or whether they emerge through reproduction from other multizoa organisms; They may also wonder what mechanisms underlie the capacity of multizoa organisms to diversify, to acquire different traits, and as we shall see, they will come up with interesting hypotheses. But before we touch upon these subjects, let us ask ourselves, what would our answers, as human beings, to these riddles be? First, in regard to how the number of multizoa organisms increased, we would conclude in this scenario that they all emerged through multizoa reproduction, starting with the descendants of our human society, because all human settlements would be established by other human settlements (with our human society as the exception to this rule). Second, in regard to the diversification of multizoa traits, we would know that it would all be made possible by the human beings that lived within generation after generation of multizoa organisms contributing to the multizoa organisms they would be part of, much like how the internet, the skyscraper, ways of harnessing electricity arose within our human society - they were developed and perfected by the hands and minds of countless people, working sometimes alone, sometimes in cooperation with one another.

We may also acknowledge that natural selection would play a role in the evolution of multizoa organisms. To understand why, let us perform another thought experiment. Imagine that human society were to suddenly reproduce on 100 different planets. As each multizoa organisms would develop, it is likely that the people who live in them would make changes here and there to the initial design, would implement various technological innovations, various ways of organizing their society, etc. and this would make each multizoa organism unique. Now, one would expect that even though all these changes would probably be done with the best of intentions, some multizoa members of this hundred batch would emerge as especially promising. And even though all multizoa organisms that would be born from our human society would inherit the reproductive system developed by our human society, so they would have an easier time reproducing, it still takes time, a lot of resources and an efficient organization for a multizoa organism to mature and for its reproduction to take place, which is why those that would be most promising would have better chances to reproduce themselves, like our human society would have done. And of course, this means that those multizoa organisms that emerge as promising would be more likely to grow in numbers sustainably within their environment – in other words, they would likely be those "naturally selected" to perpetuate their "species". Therefore, natural selection would play a role in the evolution of multizoa organisms.

So, one way to summarize all of this is by saying that multizoa life and its profusion would be made possible by the process of evolution through the natural selection of multizoa organisms that underwent teleological mutations. Teleological in this case just means purposeful mutations developed by the human beings living within multizoa organisms.

Now, let's say that after some amount of scientific investigation, the alien scientists do discover that all multizoa organisms are born through reproduction, they discover fossilized multizoa organisms spread throughout the galactic area which makes them think of a multizoa tree of life, they discover the fact that multizoa species may sometimes be set apart by only a few multizoa traits which they do not share, and stumble upon other discoveries that point them in the right direction to formulate an accurate theory of multizoa evolution. But remember that because of the difference in size and speed between us and them, and because of the limitations of their scientific instruments, they would entertain a very simplistic opinion of human beings, so they wouldn't know where the innovations that would lead to the development of new "multizoa traits" came from, from skyscrapers to the engines that propel starships. That's why, to explain the development of multizoa organisms generation after generation, they would come up with the theory of evolution through the natural selection of multizoa organisms that underwent **random** mutations, even though we know that they would in fact be purposeful mutations developed by people who have lived within generation after generation of human societies.

Now of course, to say that the human innovations which produce what the alien scientists would see as novel multizoa traits are random seems preposterous to us. If we were to be propelled to a far-off descendant of human society living eons from now on a distant planet and see that instead houses built of concrete, there would be buildings built of living biological material, and instead of vehicles running on fossil fuels, you would have flying cars running on hydrogen, and wherever there would be need for repetitive labor you would find complex automatons doing the task instead of human beings, we couldn't conceive of any random process that could have lead to the developments of all these innovations, these multizoa traits. But we must take into account the unfortunate position of the alien scientists: they are searching for a logical understanding of how novel multizoa traits are developed without having access to our human world - the words we utter vanish in the flash of an instant for them, as do our individual actions. They are limited by the capabilities of their scientific instruments, and by the difference in size and speed between us and them - we essentially live on a different order of magnitude within nature.

Now, let us look at the current theory of evolution as it applies to multicellular organisms. In its current form, it is by and large the theory of evolution through the natural selection of organisms that underwent random mutations. But if the alien scientists aren't able to find the actual source of novel multizoa mutations due to the difference in size and speed between them and us, then perhaps the same is true in relation to us and the true source of novel multicellular mutations - that is, we may see their development to be due to random factors because of the difference in size-speed between us and cells.

In fact, if we were to be the size and speed of cells and be propelled from an organism living in the beginning of multicellular life billions of years ago to the modern human body today, we would have the same "wow" reaction that we would have as humans travelling from our multizoa organism to a far-off multizoa descendant of human society. So, why would we agree with considering the evolution of cellular organism as being the result of random forces, when we wouldn't be able to do so in regard to multizoa organisms? That's why the book proposes the theory that novel traits which appear within multicellular organisms, rather than being the product of chance, are developments that arise from the contributions brought by cells to the organisms they are part of, much like how multizoa development is the result of humans contributing to the organisms they are part of.

They are multiple lines of evidence in support of this theory, from the increasing realization that cells are unique, independent, autonomous beings capable of unique action, to the complexity of multicellular organisms, to the conclusions that can be derived from the alien thought experiment.

But to be fair, the idea that randomness in the case of multicellular evolution is just a way of saying "we don't know what caused it" is not new. There are other eminent scientists which have talked about this, pointing to the incredible complexity of cellular and multicellular organisms as evidence against the "random" apparition of cellular and multicellular traits. The real innovation in In Principio Res is the approach to the explanation of why we shouldn't consider the process random, by revealing the insights that we can gain from looking at multizoa evolution through the eyes of the alien scientists.

So, to summarize it in a language that applies to both multicellular and multizoa organisms, the book proposes that the evolution of organisms takes place through the natural selection of organisms that underwent teleological mutations developed by their basic units.

## Chapter V. The Utility Of Moral Precepts

And now we can return to the utility of the moral precepts discussed.

We've mentioned earlier that human society is a protomultizoa organism, on par with the protocell, and the first multicellular organisms to have emerged within nature. And based on evidence, if we are to look at the difference between the first cell to have emerged within nature and present-day cells, like human cells for example, we find that present-day cells are much more evolved - in other words, they are more adapted to their environment, able to handle much more complex tasks, more efficient, etc. Or if we are to look at the difference between the first multicellular organisms to have emerged within nature, and present-day multicellular organisms like the human body, we find that present day multicellular organisms are much more evolved. The human being is a more evolved organism than the trilobites that lived 500 million years ago, for example, or any other organism that lived during that period to the extent that the fossil record shows their existence. At the same time, the consciousness of the first animals which appeared within nature - if we are to name it consciousness - was likely much more primitive than the consciousness of some organisms that lived today, like those of mammals in general, and of the human in particular. Based on these correlations, we can arrive at the conclusion that the multizoa organisms which will be born through reproduction from human society will come to be much more evolved then our society - in other words, the colonies that we would establish on other planets, or the starships that we would build and their descendants would come to be much more evolved, likely surpassing human society in virtually every field. Indeed, they would have at their disposal from the start all the developments that took human society centuries to develop, from ways of harnessing electricity to means of instant global communication, and they would be able to build upon them from their inception.

That being said, who knows what these multizoa organisms will come to know about everything from laws of nature to the origin of the universe? Who knows how much more evolved their technology will be? Their way of viewing the world? What new artforms they will develop?

This fact, that we are likely primitive in relation to human society's potential multizoa descendants instills a certain degree of humility, but our position also imparts a great sense of honor, because we, as a protomultizoa organism, can be the seed for the multizoa future, for a multizoa tree of life that may extend throughout the galaxies and gain a complexity beyond imagining. We've already briefly mentioned this multizoa tree during the topic of evolution, but let's talk about what it really means.

You know, when you open an introductory biology textbook, there is almost always a tree of life that classifies all the different cellular organisms - from bacteria to animal species - showing how they are related and most importantly, how they all derive from a common root. Well, at the base of this root lies the common ancestor of all cellular life - the protocell. That's where it all started from. The tree of life that you can currently find in biology textbooks refers to cellular organisms. We, on the other hand, can be the root of a multizoa tree of life, the common ancestor from which all multizoa organisms draw their lineage. Our human society can be that seed from which the multizoa tree of life will sprout, which is an incredible opportunity.

But, as hinted earlier, in order for this to happen, human society would have to develop the ability to reproduce, the bodily systems necessary for reproduction, and this is a notoriously difficult task that would require not just a few bright minds, but a lot of bright minds and a high level of cooperation between human beings found throughout human society. Presently, the goal of establishing a colony on another planet seems like a distant dream. Our human society is simply not capable of developing its multizoa reproduction system as is.

And that's where providing human beings found throughout human society with their basic necessities comes in, which among other things, would provide human beings with the environment that promotes the innovations necessary for developing human society's reproduction capabilities.

To understand why, let's look at the human body. As the culmination of human ancestor cells forming societies for billions of years, your body has a nutrient distribution system that is very efficient, which is why you do not have to eat all the time for cells throughout your body to get the glucose that they need, or you don't have to breathe as if you are running a marathon so that cells throughout your body get the oxygen that they require. This nutrient distribution system ensures that the cells all over your body have their basic necessities met as long as those nutrients exist in the body - in other words, as long as you eat properly. This, among other things, is what allows your cells, including your nervous cells, to do their thing without having to focus a large amount of time and energy upon satisfying their basic necessities individually.

However, imagine for a moment that your nervous cells would have to forage their basic necessities individually from their environment. What would happen?

It was postulated earlier that the cells of your nervous system synthesize the elements (e.g. ideas, feelings, sensations) which can become part of your conscious awareness. But for them to actually deal with synthesizing these elements, or to turn their attention to the most deserving elements that are made available by their neighboring cells, these cells have to be specialized in the relevant fields. As an analogy with human society, in order for a human or a group of people to make a high quality movie, they need to have certain information, certain abilities that differ from those required to make a high quality book - abilities that develop in time, with practice. The same goes for nervous cells: They need time and practice to develop abilities which lead to the synthesis of the varied array of elements which emerge within one's consciousness. And one factor that plays a big role in the time-availability necessary to follow these specializations is that these cells have their basic necessities satisfied through the efficient nutrient distribution system mentioned. To put it in human terms, human cells don't have to "worry about" where they get their "bread" tomorrow, and so they are liberated from having to acquire specializations that are linked to that worry, and instead have the freedom to follow specializations like those of nervous cells, which allow them to do things like collectively think about the organism they are part of as a whole.

However, imagine for a moment that the body's nutrient distribution system doesn't exist, or that it is very inefficient. As a consequence, instead of growing in conditions of abundance and having the time and necessary resources to contribute to your conscious awareness, the cells within your nervous system would have to focus on ensuring their basic necessities individually from their environment, like glucose and oxygen, in order to survive. To ensure those basic necessities, they would have to acquire the specializations that would enable them to do so, that would allow them to forage those resources from their environment, and not specializations that would allow them to synthesize elements that may become thoughts within your consciousness, or they would perish otherwise. So, if they would have had to ensure their basic necessities individually, the stem cells that became nervous cells would have acquired other specializations, and would have engaged in other activities that don't have as much to do with the synthesis of thoughts. And without cells to engage in such activities, your cognitive capacity would be null, would disappear, the consciousness of your body would cease to exist. In the fortunate case that some sporadic cells would still be able to synthesize relevant elements, your thoughts would be like the flickers of light emitted by a small population of fireflies amidst a large forest. In other words, you would likely have a thought once in a while, and a truly interesting thought probably rarer than that.

Fortunately, our nature is not that way, which is why we can have a rich mental life, but whereas the human body is the culmination of human ancestor cells for billions of years, our present human society is the first of its kind. And looking within human society, we find that human beings have to allocate a large portion of their time and resources towards acquiring their basic necessities. This takes a toll on the cognitive capacity of human society - that is, on the contributions brought by human beings to the organism they are part of.

Takes a toll how? Like it was mentioned before, in the together-knowing theory of consciousness, an organism's consciousness is comprised of whatever the organism's basic units and networks of basic units focus upon collectively. So, human society's consciousness can be considered the elements synthesized by human beings that they focus upon collectively - the books, movies, video games, shows, inventions that are very popular. Therefore, it follows that the more people focus upon an element, the more human society is sharply focused upon that element.

And like we've said before, whatever we focus upon collectively is important, because it grows in various ways - it gets funded, it gets distributed, it gets implemented, it gets analyzed, it inspires the synthesis of related elements and so on, depending on the nature of the element of course. But the fact that presently human beings within human society have to acquire their basic necessities individually means for many humans that they have to acquire whatever specializations are made available to them by their environment, many of which require much time and cognitive resources and are unrelated to the synoptic perspective of human society. As such, to ask people to focus sustainably on human society as a whole, to contribute in unique ways to the collective focus of human beings, to seek to spread the elements that they feel holds promise throughout human society or to help develop the reproductive capabilities of human society seems misplaced for a large population of humans that have more immediate concerns, even more so when we take into account the fact that many people have not just themselves, but a family that they have to look after as well, for whose basic necessities and possibility to thrive they are responsible.

That's how this situation is taking a toll on human society's cognitive abilities, so then, the idea is to follow the example of multicellular organisms, which have been sculpted by generations upon generations of multicellular evolution through natural selection, and seek to provide human beings found throughout human society with their basic necessities.

To put it differently, let's return to the goal of developing human society's reproduction capabilities: We don't know where the human being that has the potential to develop the concept for the engine that will eventually come to power the first starship will come from, or other such inventions with far-reaching effects - we don't know who these people will be, or where such people will be born. But what we can be sure of is that if such people don't have their basic necessities met, they are likely to concentrate their time and energy towards ensuring those basic necessities, upon acquiring skills relating to this endeavor, and not nurturing their potential to develop to such things as the engine we've mentioned.

It's similar to the fact that you don't know which part of your brain, which cell or cellular network will come to synthesize the next good idea that will pop into your head, or the solution to the problem you are facing, which is why you have 86 billion neurons in the brain alone, well fed, taken care of, and kept happy to the best of your abilities - or more accurately, it's why the process of multicellular evolution through natural selection that has taken place over countless generations has revealed this to be the most successful body plan.

And like the next good idea you will have or the next solution to the problem you face could make you happy, as the consciousness of your body - which in the together-knowing theory of consciousness means that it would make the general population of cells within your nervous system happy - so too might the discovery of the engine I was talking about lead to the general happiness of human beings of all shapes and sizes living within human society - in other words, to the happiness of human society.

But at the same time, it takes a lot of brain power to find a solution to a complex problem that you meet, and it will take a lot of human power to overcome the technological and organizatorial challenges linked to the development of human society's capacity to reproduce.

That's why the book recommends offering human beings their basic necessities: it will give them time to think of how to achieve this, as well of as other things that are about human society as a whole - in the same way that your nervous cells have time, energy, the resources to contribute to your conscious thoughts - and this would benefit everybody, all human beings.

Now, when I say "offer human beings throughout human society their basic necessities unconditionally", I don't mean to do it in just any way...but to make it a well-thought action. There are for example models of autonomous homes, which can offer shelter, electricity, water, sewage and even food without them having to be connected to a centralized grid, with a minimal cost both financially and for the planet. A good example of such homes is the Earthship model, developed by Michael Reynolds and his team. Of course, these types of homes are still at their early stages of development, but the more they would be built, the more they would be improved, be made more efficient, more comfortable, etc. The people that would build them would come up with new ideas, new systems, like it happens in any field. In other words, these models of homebuilding would arise within the collective focus of human beings - human society would think of them, and with time, this thinking process would improve them, in the same way that the ideas which arise within your consciousness, when you apply them and then you consider how they turned out, you may improve.

And if these types of homes would be built on a widespread scale, people would always have a basis...they wouldn't have to worry about their basic necessities, they could focus towards other aspects of life. And on this basis, we could build anything else, up until acquiring human society's capacity to reproduce.

But of course, providing human beings throughout human society with their basic necessities sustainably to increase the cognitive capacity of human society isn't just about accomplishing the goal of developing human society's reproductive capabilities, just like having 86 billion neurons to support your consciousness isn't just about solving the problems that you encounter...To have a rich, varied mental life as a human, as a multicellular organism is useful in so many other ways, which I'm sure you can attest to. And the same would apply to human society's conscious life - it would be useful in many ways for the humans and human networks within human society to have human society's conscious life be varied and rich. It's about the "little" things too. In fact, if the first moral principle was to be generally adopted and people would seek to contribute to human society's consciousness as they would like for the cells of their bodies to contribute to their individual consciousnesses, then the more people alive the merrier, because it would potentially mean more diverse contributions to human society's conscious capabilities; Just like more nervous cells seem to produce more cognitive brain power.

Now, this may all seem a bit idealist, utopic, but really, the idea is for the collective focus of human beings to have the same use in relation to human society as your consciousness has for your body - you, as the consciousness of your body, generally keep in mind the well-being of the general population of cells within it. Whether you are seeking happiness, your own personal well-being, or in more extreme cases, basic necessities like food an water, at the basis of these desires lies the well-being of the cells within your body. This is the result of billions of years of cellular evolution. So then, based on these lessons imparted by multicellular nature, the collective attention of human beings should keep in mind the well-being of the general population of human beings within human society.

In other words, if we as human beings seek to make the world we are a better place for the greatest number of cells within our bodies through our own individual consciousness, and if this setup yields such good results for our individual survival and thriving, then we should learn from this and seek to make the world we are part of a better place for the greatest number of people through the consciousness of human society - that is, through the collective focus of human beings - in order to ensure the survival and prospering of human society.

# Chapter VI.Counterarguments

As mentioned before, the moral precepts described do not have a metaphysical, but an entirely materialistic fundament. That is to say, they should be pursued because they are **logical and useful.**

Some however may like to challenge their utility by saying that it's not universal, that some people living within human society, mostly those who now have a lot of power and influence, enjoy a very good life which extends to their family and loved ones precisely by not following these moral precepts, but by running counter to them, people who would stand to lose if say, human beings throughout human society would have their basic necessities met unconditionally.

But that is true only from a very narrow, short-term perspective. To better understand why, ask yourself: Would you have prefer it for your descendants to have lived as kings in 13$^{th}$ century Europe, or as relatively prosperous middle-class people in contemporary society?

And to put this question in perspective, let us take the example of king Edward the First of England - which ruled England in the 13$^{th}$ century - and his family. Living in palaces, enjoying good food, clean water, and an extensive body of servants, king Edward's family had a most luxurious lifestyle compared to that of common folk in medieval Europe. However, historical records show that from the 16 children Queen Eleanor bore the king, 10 of them died during childhood, with only 6 managing to live beyond age 11. Of those, only three lived beyond the age of forty, despite the royal family having the best doctors of the time at their disposal. That's because medicine was primitive in that period, unable to do much to keep the children of even the most affluent members of society safe. Fast forward to today, and, thanks to contributions brought these past centuries by human beings living throughout human society, many of the diseases to which children succumbed in former times are no longer challenging the offspring of the average person in the industrialized world. Moreover, life expectancy has doubled, from mid-thirties to about 64 years worldwide. But medicine was not the only human field that can be considered primitive during that time compared to how it is today. So were the other sciences, the arts, technology. The quality of life has improved markedly, with a great many more possibilities in virtually all aspects of human life made generally available to people of all classes. As a consequence, though they were royalty, the quality of life, the scope of their horizon, the possibilities that King Edward and his family had at their disposal as human beings were quite limited compared to those of even the middle-class person in industrialized society living today. Among other things was their lack of understanding the world around them: they had no knowledge of the laws of nature like gravity, the composition of stars, atoms, cells, etc…One could say that they were ignorant, but, of course, due to of no fault of their own…the human contributions that amassed to the present day knowledge of the world which we use to alleviate our ignorance however slightly simply weren't there.

So then, applying this question to present-day possibilities, would you like for your descendants to have a lot of power and influence within the organism that we are part of as it is at this stage of development, or would you rather them be "middle-class" in an organism that would be as different from ours as human society in the 13th century was from our present day society? What do you think they would prefer? The answer may very well be the latter, however at this stage in human society's development, in order for the difference between our world and that of our descendants to be the same as the difference between the world of 13$^{th}$ century Europe and that of ours, human beings would have to work together, as one organism. And in particular, because it is only through a massive, large-scale, long-term operation which would include human beings found throughout human society that we would be able to develop human society's ability to reproduce.

Also regarding their utility, one of the moral precepts that we've mentioned before was "Do unto the collective focus of human beings as you would have the cells of your body do onto the consciousness of your cellular society." which, as we've said, points to the fact that if you want for the cells of your body to synthesize and help elevate within your conscious awareness elements that, in a word, help make the organism you are a better place for the greatest number of your cells, then so should you seek to aid in the synthesis and in the elevation within the collective focus of human beings elements that, in a word, help make the organism we are all part of a better place for the greatest number of human beings.

What this means is that if these moral precepts are generally adopted, then more elements synthesized by humans which have the potential to make the world a better place for the greatest number of human beings will emerge within our collective focus, will become very popular, and will be thus nurtured and put to use through that popularity.

Now, as a side note, making the world a better place is more of a technical term used within In Principio Res. It means to combine the unique possibilities you are provided by your environment, the unique information you have gathered, the unique abilities you have acquired throughout your lifetime in order to seek to help make the world a better place for the greatest number of human beings in a way that is pleasurable for and unique to you. Its origins stem from the first moral principle, which as mentioned before, says that if you want for your cells to synthesize and elevate within your consciousness elements that make the world you are a better place for the greatest number of your cells, so too should you seek to synthesize and elevate within the collective focus of human beings elements that make the world a better place for the greatest number of people, and much like the former scenario benefits the cells throughout your body, the latter scenario would benefit humans throughout human society. So, a writer for example may write a story that he thinks may help make the world a better place. A businessman may use his business knowledge to start a venture that he thinks may help to make the world a better place. A builder may help design a house that he thinks may help make the world a better place, and so on. In other words, if you agree with these moral precepts, it's not about trying to change your life to help make the world a better place - that's just one option - but it's about focusing your unique way of being to bring a unique contribution to this goal, putting your unique creative angle into it. Some may work on such projects alone, some may do it in groups. The theory goes that eventually, some of these contributions will help make the world a better place, just like some of the contributions your cells bring to your stream of thoughts when you are consciously focusing upon achieving a goal help you achieve the goal in question. Through our diverse contributions, making the world we are all part of a better place for the greatest number of human beings will effectively become human society's conscious goal. It is a constructive way to apply the knowledge that human society has a consciousness, and to practice human society's conscious capabilities so that they may improve - because as we know, everything gets better with practice.

So, the utility of these moral principles, and their encouragement to find a way to provide human beings with their basic necessities is generally desirable not only because it will help to achieve the long-term goal of multizoa reproduction and thus help multizoa organisms evolve, but also because short-term, it will nurture the synthesis and funding of elements that have the potential to help make the world a better place in novel, unpredictable ways for all human beings, regardless of wealth, social status, race, creed, etc., including the people living within human society who some believe are in fact better off precisely by not following these moral precepts.

And since we're on the subject, apart from their utility, the logical foothold of these moral precepts has one special subpoint for those with a lot of power and influence:

In the book, it is described how there are certain cells within the human body that have more power and influence than any other, like the insulin-producing cells in the pancreas, the endocrine cells of the thyroid gland, the dopamine-producing cells in the substantia nigra, or the nervous cells in the locus ceruleus, which have projections in nearly the whole nervous system. When these cells do not perform their task properly, diseases on the level of the entire human body can appear, including acromegaly, diabetes, Parkinson's, etc. Knowing this, one, as the consciousness of one's body, would likely want for these cells to do the task that they've been assigned, so that one's body is healthy and one's consciousness can focus on other matters than finding solutions to health issues.

In much the same way, there are certain human beings within human society that have more power and influence than most people (regardless of whether it is acquired, inherited, etc.). This includes people with a lot of wealth (In fact, in the book, money is described as a societal hormone, and it says that just like there are endocrine cells within your body that release hormones like insulin and human growth hormone, there are certain people within human society tasked with synthesizing the money hormone in the right quantities and places and releasing it into the world.) It also includes political figures and other people with a lot of influence. When these people do not use that wealth or influence properly, human society can experience phenomena that may be considered multizoa diseases, like the dot-com crash, housing bubble, economic depression, etc.

The moral precepts described here say that if the consciousness of these people would like for the cells of their respective bodies that have a lot of power and influence to use their position to the benefit of the general population of their neighboring cells, then they should do the same within human society - that is, they should use their power and influence and\or wealth to the benefit of the general population of human beings- because the two precepts are equivalent.

However, these are just the logical and utility-related reasons for why even those which may presently considered better off precisely by not following these moral precepts should follow them. It does not mean that those who do not follow them should be damnable, or scorned. Seeing human society as an organism, seeing consciousness as the collective focus of human beings, seeing the utility of acting for the well-being of all human beings did not exist in this form up until now, it is a perspective of the world that was not available, so the fact that some people do not follow these moral guidelines - and more importantly, that some people have pursued human specializations that, by agreeing with the ultimate conclusion of moral relativism, are in contrast with these moral guidelines, with all the habits that they've acquired in the process, is understandable.

At the same time, any human being that has tried to change one's habits knows that it is not easy to achieve, so any mature person of this generation that, following the logic of seeing human society as an organism, seeks to change one's habits in order to agree with the moral conclusions revealed is commendable, rather than those who will still stick to their habits if they are in contrast with these conclusions being damnable. It is human nature to stick to what you know. The next generations will have a much easier time of seeing the value of these conclusions objectively, for they may become aware of them before they will have acquired habits that stand in contrast with these moral guidelines.

# Chapter VII. Conclusion

So, how can we best summarize this analysis?

Well, let's start with consciousness. Simply put, your consciousness is comprised of the information-based elements - thoughts, ideas, feelings, sensations - synthesized by your nervous cells and cellular networks that they focus upon collectively, similar to the information-based elements synthesized by human beings - books, videos, songs, etc. that become very popular within human society. This is called the together knowing-theory of consciousness. From here, a science of consciousness can be put together by studying the popular elements within human society and their connection to human beings, and juxtaposing this study with the conscious thoughts, ideas, feelings, sensations emerging within one's conscious awareness, and their connection to individual nervous cells and cellular networks.

In regard to morality, you are the consciousness of one organism - your human body - whose thoughts and actions arise from the actions, interactions, choices of its basic units - your cells; While at the same time, you are a basic unit within another organism - human society - with your actions, interactions, contributions, choices giving rise and influencing this organism's conscious thoughts and actions.

From this, two fundamental moral principles can be extracted: Do unto your neighbor as you would have the cells of your body do unto their neighboring cells, and do unto the collective focus of human beings as you would have the cells of your body do unto the consciousness of your cellular society, because simply put, you are to human society what a cell within your body is to you.

Regarding evolution, there appears to be good reason to think that multicellular evolution is largely driven by teleological mutations developed by cells and sculpted by natural selection, but more importantly, we've seen that human society is a multizoa organism, the first of its kind, and that multizoa organisms may evolve over generations just like multicellular organisms did. But for that to happen, our human society would have to develop the ability to reproduce. Really, this seems to be the exam that nature has laid in front our multizoa organism: Will we, as the basic units and networks of basic units of this organism, be able to learn how to cooperate in useful time in order to develop this organism's ability to reproduce? It is a tough exam, but the benefits of passing it are unmeasurable, for if we do, we will become the first member in a multizoa phylogenetic tree that may spread into eternity. All human disagreements seem to fade in comparison to this goal, do they not?

However, this task is not one to be tackled with by a few bright minds, but by a lot of bright minds. Or to put it differently, not by a nascent multizoa consciousness, but by a healthy, mature multizoa consciousness, that has gained some experience with how to think up solutions to complex problems and implement them. And in order for such a healthy, mature multizoa consciousness to arise, we would have to begin with the basics - providing human beings throughout human society with their basic necessities sustainably and unconditionally is a good start - and lay the fundamental groundwork onto which it can be constructed.

And If we do succeed in developing human society's reproduction system, we may not end up being the multizoa organisms that explains the origin of the universe, or the multizoa organism that invents instant interstellar space travel, or the multizoa organism

that invents organic means of transportation, but we would have our place of honor within the phylogeny of multizoa organisms through at least three accomplishments:
1. Being the first multizoa organism to have arisen within nature. 2. providing human beings throughout human society with their basic necessities efficiently and 3. Developing the multizoa organism's ability to reproduce.

Now, to end this conclusion on a different note, there's one more logical reason why a person should help human society as a whole thrive, and that reason is reciprocity. You see, whatever you acquire from within human society, whether they are cars, words, clothes, ideas, come from the people around you. But each such thing, as simple as it seems, was likely shaped by the hands and minds of countless human beings living throughout time within human society in order to acquire its current form. A car for example was developed by countless human beings. A new word you learn likely has its origins other languages. The designer of an article of clothing you buy was inspired by others, and used the materials made available by yet others, and so on. The point is that there's no single human being who made the things that we cherish the most, whether they are poetry made by stringing words, or cars built by shaping metal - the more accurate perspective is that each element we have at our disposal from within human society was made by human society as a whole.

Now, let's assume that whatever you willfully acquire from within human society, you do so because it provides you with happiness and well-being - whether it's a video game, a book, a car, a song. But if that happiness and well-being was made possible by human society as a whole, should you not repay it in kind, by whenever possible contributing to the happiness and well-being of the organism of human society? Food for thought.

# Part 2: Papers

## Author's Note

As mentioned in the introduction, the second part of the book is comprised of a series of papers - four, to be exact - with self-revealing titles.

The first three are sister papers - That is, what is written in one builds upon the concepts laid down in the other. Because they were each considered for publication separately, a preface was written within the latter two papers of the three with quotes from the first paper, so as to introduce the reader to the crucial concepts it contained. After considering it, I've decided to keep the preface in both, so that anyone who wishes to read only one paper of the three can do so unencumbered. Also, that way, if one wished, one could tear from the book the pages that contain any one paper, and nevertheless understand what is being said. (Though why anyone would want to do so is unknown). If you read the papers one after the other in the order they were placed in the book however (which is recommended), you may skip the preface if you so wish.

The fourth paper, "Is human society a multizoa organism?", is standalone. It was included because the concept of multizoa organisms, though essential in understanding all the other ideas put forth in this book, was treated somewhat sparingly in the rest of the work. It is a short paper at 10 pages, simple to understand, but nonetheless I find that it brings substantial insights to the topic.

Each of the four papers delve somewhat deeper than the first part of the book into their particular subject, therefore much of what was said in the first part will be repeated in these papers, though perhaps from a different angle and at times supplemented by other ideas. Yet, by reading both the first part and the second part of the book, considering the different approaches, the reader will have probably familiarized himself with the concepts this book contains well enough, which is the main aim.

# CAN CONSCIOUS THOUGHTS BE CONSIDERED "WORKS OF ART" CREATED BY CELLS, MUCH LIKE HOW MOVIES, BOOKS, VIDEO GAMES ARE WORKS OF ART CREATED BY PEOPLE?

The main scientific paradigm in respect to thoughts is that they are electrochemical patterns arising in the brain from the activity of nervous cells,[1] which (though not wrong per se) is not very revealing in terms of how the activity of single cells and small cellular networks are connected to consciousness. In this paper, it will be argued that a person's thoughts are in fact elements (e.g. particular ideas, sounds, images, etc.) made by the person's nervous cells and cellular networks that have the necessary qualities to attract their collective attention, not unlike how some of the books, movies, songs made by human beings are read\watched\listened to by human beings found throughout human society and thus they become very well-known, very popular; Evidence for this thesis will be provided, potential objections addressed, and then we will proceed to show how this novel approach to the nature of thoughts solves some of the fundamental questions that arise in the study of consciousness.

---

[1] Elizabeth Dougherty. (April 26, 2011). What Are Thoughts Made Of? Retrieved from http://engineering.mit.edu/ ask/what-are-thoughts-made

# I. Introduction

For a long time since microscopes enabled their initial discovery, cells have been generally regarded as no more than simple clog-like machines, or at most, molecular factories.[2]

But with continuous improvements in microscope design, in methods of recording cellular activity and in cellular staining techniques, there has been increasing consensus starting with the end of the 20th century that rather then being mindless drones, cells (we are placing an emphasis on nervous cells in this paper) are in fact unique, independent, oftentimes unpredictable entities. Modern evidence in support of this theory can be found in our present understanding of just how varied and complex cellular means of communication are[3], the vast amount of new nervous cell types that are being discovered[4], the ever increasing pallet of factors that we learn are influencing cellular actions[5], etc. (For more on this, you may visit Jon Lieff's excellent blog on the subject.[6])

Cells are much smaller than humans. Cells move much faster than humans as well (again, we are placing an emphasis on nervous cells,

---

[2] See Edwin W. Taylor, Thomas D. Pollard (Feb 2001) *E.B. Wilson Lecture: The Cell as Molecular Machine* for an example. Retrieved from http://www.ncbi.nlm.nih.gov/pmc/articles/PMC30940/

[3] Jon Lieff (September 21, 2014 )*The Remarkable Language of Cells*. Retrieved from http://jonlieffmd.com/ blog/the-remarkable-language-of-cells

[4] Jon Lieff (October 12, 2014 ) *How Many Different Kinds of Neurons Are There*. Retrieved from http://jonlieffmd.com/blog/how-many-different-kinds-of-neurons-are-there

[5] Jon Lieff (October 19, 2014 ) *Does Activity Determine Synaptic Creation and Pruning* Retrieved from http://jonlieffmd.com/blog/does-activity-determine-synaptic-creation-and-pruning

[6] http://jonlieffmd.com/

which are known to be able to send upwards of a hundred nervous impulses every second) - but that's true only when interpreting things from our human perspective. It doesn't mean that cells are small, or that they move very fast from the perspective of a cell - indeed, given the fact that cellular action & communication have to be very precise despite the microscopic area in which they unfold and their impressive speed by human standards, evidence points to the contrary. There will be more said on the matter of temporal relativity throughout the paper, but for the sake of the argument, entertain this assumption from this point: That a day passing from the perspective of a human being can equal to a year's passing from the perspective of a cell. (Again, emphasis on nervous cells.)

A paradigm shift on thoughts: As mentioned in the paper's abstract, thoughts have been traditionally regarded as patterns of electrochemical activity arising within the brain, which (though not wrong per se) doesn't tell us much about how the activity of single cells and small cellular networks are connected to consciousness. However, we are now entertaining the idea outlined in the first paragraph, that cells are unique, independent, oftentimes unpredictable entities[7], and the idea outlined in paragraph two, that a day passing from the perspective of a human being can equal to a year from the perspective of a cell. So, let us pose the question: **What if thoughts are elements synthesized by cells and cellular networks within a person's nervous system, much like how books and movies are elements synthesized by human beings within human society?** And what if those thoughts that emerge within a person's conscious awareness are in fact the elements synthesized

---

[7] This however should not be taken to mean that cells are individualistic in the same way as humans are- they are obviously not. This subject will be approached in Chapter VI of this paper.

by the cells\cellular networks within that person's nervous system that attract their collective attention? Similar to how certain movies, songs, books (videos of cats playing the piano...basically, any element that has its essence in the information it carries, rather than its physical basis) synthesized by human beings within human society have the necessary qualities to attract the collective attention of people and become very popular.

*Note: "Collective attention" may sometimes be referred to as "collective focus" (as in "collective focus of cells and cellular networks", or "collective focus of human beings"). The two terms may be used interchangeably.*

In the next chapter, we will begin to offer some intriguing evidence for this theory. Following that, we will address a possible counterargument, and then we will proceed to reinforce the validity of this perspective with the help of a thought experiment that will yield a number of informative analogies.

## II. The Collective Focus Effect

One important line of evidence which supports the approach to consciousness formulated in the last chapter is the fact that when something attracts the collective attention of human beings (i.e. it becomes very popular), elements that relate to that thing may emerge within their collective focus as a result, as this is similar to one of the most fundamental effects of human conscious focus: When one consciously focuses upon something, one may subsequently notice thoughts\elements that relate to that thing emerging within one's consciousness.

To expand upon the subject, when you think about something, you find elements synthesized by your cells - creative ideas, feelings, images - that relate to your object of focus emerging within your conscious awareness. For example, the solutions that you come up with when you start consciously focusing upon a problem.

With that in mind, what happens when human beings focus upon something collectively? Well, new elements which relate to that thing are synthesized by human beings throughout human society. For example, a very popular movie may spark scintillating articles, blog posts, fan art, talk show episodes, documentaries, TV show-spinoffs. Then, some of these elements may have the necessary qualities – may be useful enough, or relevant enough, or insightful enough, or interesting enough to be assimilated by a large number of human beings and emerge within their collective focus, restarting the process just described. Take for example M*A*S*H. This successful movie with 5 Oscar nominations (drawn from a less-successful book) inspired the synthesis of the TV series that went by the same name, which surpassed in popularity that initial movie. In fact, it became so popular that the finale had the highest rating of any show finale up until that time. (1983) There can also be found examples of popular books inspiring the synthesis of movies[8], movies inspiring the synthesis of books[9], movies inspiring the synthesis of songs[10], video games inspiring the synthesis of movies[11], academic papers inspiring the synthesis of cartoons[12],

---

[8] e.g. Hunger Games movie series inspired by the books of the same name.
[9] e.g. Matrix and Philosophy book inspired by the Matrix movie series.
[10] e.g. Vanessa Carlton - Ordinary Day inspired by Disney's Peter Pan.
[11] e.g. Prince of Persia: Sands Of Time movie inspired by the Prince of Persia video game series.

etc. and some of the results of these inspirations become more popular than the element they were inspired from. This is not unlike how, if one rummages through one's memory, one may surely find examples of conscious feelings inspiring the emergence of words within one's consciousness, words of feelings, images of words, words of images, sounds of images, etc.

So, to conclude, when human beings focus upon something collectively, elements may subsequently emerge within their collective focus that relate to that thing, as it happens with the thoughts\elements that emerge within one's conscious focus. And if we are to juxtapose the two phenomena, the reason why when one consciously focuses upon something, related elements (thoughts, feelings, sensations) emerge within one's conscious awareness is because cells and cellular networks within one's nervous system synthesize elements that relate to that object of focus, some of which have the necessary qualities to attract their collective attention and thus emerge within one's conscious awareness.

This theory is also in agreement with one of the most established scientific premises regarding consciousness: That rather than being the product of a particular area of the brain, conscious processes are decentralized, with consciousness arising from the interactions taking place between nervous cells and cellular networks found throughout the nervous system.[13]

---

[12] e.g. Cartoons inspired by Thomas Nagel's paper "What it's like to be a bat?".
[13] Bernard J. Baars *et al (2003)* Brain, Conscious Experience And The Observing Self.

## III. Time's Passing

One reason why it may seem strange to consider thoughts as "elements synthesized by one's cells" is because from a human being's perspective, one's thoughts can oftentimes seem to emerge practically instantly in response to what one focuses upon (for example, a potential solution to a problem one has just encountered may surface within one's consciousness just moments after one consciously considers the problem in question) or to changes within one's environment, so there seems to be no time for a process of synthesis to underscore the development of one's thoughts. That's why entertaining the idea that time can move much slower from the perspective of a cell is important: Because it gets rid of the anthropocentric view of time's passing, and gives an account of how a thought can appear to emerge seemingly instantly from one's conscious perspective, while at the same time be something of a work of art patiently synthesized by one's cells.

For one's consciousness, thoughts may be seen as emerging very fast because essentially one's consciousness *is* those thoughts, and so the speed of their emergence within one's awareness is as fast as one can think.

## IV. Thought Experiment: The Alien Scientists

Based upon the points made thus far, we may entertain the possibility that **a human's conscious focus is essentially comprised of the elements synthesized by that human's nervous cells and networks of nervous cells that have the necessary qualities to attract their collective attention** (e.g. particular ideas, feelings, sensations, etc.), **and that this conscious focus is not unlike the collective attention of human beings within human society**, which is essentially comprised of elements synthesized by human beings and human networks (e.g. songs, books, movies...any element whose essence lies in the information it carries, rather than its physical basis) that have the necessary qualities to become very popular within human society. This is the together-knowing theory of consciousness.

But are we able to offer further evidence in favor of this theory? To address this question, entertain the following thought experiment:

Imagine that a group of very large extraterrestrials (each one roughly the size of Earth), and also very slow (for whom a human year would be the equivalent to the timespan of merely a day) travel among the galaxies, when their spaceship discovers a "strange fluorescence" emanating from the surface of a planet they're passing by. As a consequence, large as they are, they approach this planet - which of course is in fact Earth - and unexpectedly discover human society growing on it. Also imagine that it's the first time they encounter anything remotely resembling human society in their entire history of space explorations. They are in fact extremely different beings from us. In their situation, how would they define human society? From their perspective (so large and so...slow) they would see human society as a whole - as kind of a moss-like organism streaked along Earth's surface (not unlike how a human being sees the human body as a unified whole, even though we know it to be made up of cells). Despite the fact that they would be looking at human society, these extraterrestrials wouldn't be able to perceive individual humans at first, because for them, human beings would be of a microscopic size.

Let's imagine however that these are science prone lifeforms, so they use microscopes, endoscopes and so on to analyze this "being" growing on Earth's surface down to its "microscopic" structure...and they discover the existence of humans. Following a healthy degree of observation, would they not proclaim us in the end the fundamental structural and functional units of human society, responsible for such things as human society's metabolism, the growth of its body, etc., just like how we've defined the cell as the fundamental structural and functional unit of the human body? From their perspective, they probably would.

But at the same time, would these humongous and slow aliens not have a very simplistic view of humans, due to extremely limited information they (and their instruments) can pick up from complex human action because of the difference in size and speed between them and us? For example, they wouldn't be able to decode human speech; A person holding a one hour monologue would be compressed in time for the alien scientists to an instant...to a "sound impulse" at most, if their instruments would be equipped with the ability to pick up human speech at all. This is much like how we interpret electrical/electrochemical interactions taking place between nervous cells as "nervous impulses", rather than cellular speech, or anything as complex as that. In other words, the perspective of the alien scientists is becoming very similar to our human perspective of cells.

Now, back to the idea that human consciousness is similar to the collective focus of human beings. Say that the alien scientists somehow develop a "human society" imaging device that allows them to view the extent to which an element synthesized by humans travels throughout human society (book, movie, mp3 song, etc...) even though they wouldn't be able to decode the contents of the element in question. How would they perceive for example the distribution of a book that becomes very popular within human society, from the beginning of that travel, to its peak, all the way to its end? Well, from their size and speed, they would probably see it as a wave of activity that starts small (from where the book begins its initial distribution) and then spreads throughout human society (as it is being read by more and more people, passed along, etc.) Well, at present, one of the most well-documented and established neuronal correlates of consciousness is that whenever a thought becomes conscious, brain imaging devices (such as the fMRI and the MEG) record a massive wave of activity coursing throughout the brain[14], much like how the alien scientists would record their own "wave of activity" within human society as the book becomes more and more popular. Moreover, from the size and speed of the alien scientists, this wave of activity coursing within human society would be perceived as unfolding quite fast, much like how human scientists perceive a wave of activity coursing through the brain when a thought becomes conscious as unfolding very fast. And this is just one line of evidence that points to just how deep the juxtaposition between human consciousness and the collective focus of human beings goes.

---

[14] Stanislas Dahene, *Consciousness and the Brain: Deciphering How the Brain Codes Our Thoughts.*

# V. The Potency Of The Analogy

One may make the case that several analogies similar to the one between alien scientists and humans described in the third chapter exist, and that they have often proven to have their limits. For example, electrons orbiting the nucleus of an atom have often been paralleled to planets orbiting the sun, thus comparing solar systems to atoms, but that two systems are set apart by a great many differences which stand out upon closer inspection.

However, that doesn't mean that some analogies do not reveal more (i.e. are not more faithful to the object of analogy) than others. To illustrate the potency of the analogy between the alien scientists' relationship to a human and a human's relationship to a cell, imagine that the alien scientists decide to send an asteroid towards Earth, though from a safe distance to emulate a natural occurrence, and just stand back to observe the results. And let's say that our astronomers observe the asteroid in safe time, and that we eventually decide to send a missile to obliterate it. Would the alien scientists, due to their size and speed, not interpret the sending of the missile as **the action of human society**, rather than the result of countless human beings that were involved in such a defense response? And isn't this much like how we for example interpret catching a ball during a play of catch as the action of the human being playing, even though we know that the person's body is in fact made up of countless cells, which are acting in concert to catch the ball? It is just natural from the human size and speed to interpret things that way in the latter case, in the same way that it is natural from the size and speed of the alien scientists to interpret the sending of the missile as the action of human society. [15]

# VI. The Homunculus Fallacy

As has been mentioned, because of the size and speed difference between them and humans, the alien scientists would interpret the missile sent from within human society to destroy the asteroid they flung towards Earth as **the action of human society**, rather than the result of countless human beings that were involved in such a challenging defense response….It would just be natural for them to interpret things that way. Following that, let's say that the missile reaches its target and destroys the asteroid. How would the alien scientists interpret this success? Well, they might conclude that the organism that is human society is aware of its environment and is able to act based on what it perceives. In other words, they may conclude that this organism growing on the surface of Earth is conscious to a certain degree, although from their perspective, they wouldn't be able to tell exactly how this consciousness arises from the activity of single human beings.

But at the same time, would one say that human society, when looked at from the perspective of the alien scientists is conscious in the same way that we consider a human being to be conscious? No, of course not, and through the together-knowing theory of consciousness we can flesh out the differences between the two types of consciousnesses. For example, the elements that would

---

[15] A more in depth account of the alien scientists thought experiment and its many uses, as well an explanation as to why it is such a potent analogy to a human's relationship with a cell can be found in the book *In Principio Res* by Narcis Marincat (2014), from which this paper draws its inspiration.

emerge within the collective focus of human beings[16] to mobilize their coordinated action in the defense response against the asteroid would be books, news stories, documentaries, military operation orders - in short, elements that can be synthesized by human beings and human networks. By contrast, the elements that emerge within the collective focus of a human being's cells (i.e. that human's consciousness) in order to mobilize their coordinated action of catching the ball while playing catch are images, ideas, possibly imagined sounds - in other words, elements that can be synthesized by cells and cellular networks.

That being said, to make the case that cells are "unique, independent, oftentimes unpredictable entities" should not be taken to mean that cells are conscious, at least not like the human beings that they form are conscious.[17] The elements synthesized by cells and cellular networks that emerge within their collective focus\one's conscious focus are those that can be synthesized by cells, whereas elements that travel within the cell that we may speculate are able to emerge within the collective focus of that cell's basic units (molecules) are those that can be synthesized by molecules and molecular networks [18], and the latter may be much simpler, or at least of a very different nature than the former.

This explanation was made to refute outright the possibility that this account of consciousness is a homunculus fallacy. [The homunculus fallacy accounts for a phenomenon in terms of the very

---

[16] i.e. what from the perspective of the alien scientists may be considered human society's conscious focus.
[17] Rather, it should be taken to mean first of all that cells are capable of doing what modern scientific investigations reveal that they can do, as exemplified by the links provided in the footnotes of the first paragraph.
[18] Again, we are referring to elements that have their essence in the information they carry, rather than their physical basis.

phenomenon that it is supposed to explain. That is, homuncular arguments are fallacious for the same reason that a recipe for cake that had as one of its ingredients 'cake' would not be considered a real recipe.[19]]

However in the case of this explanation of the origin of thoughts, rather than it being a situation where one is saying that one of the ingredients in making cake is "cake", it is more of a situation in which one of the ingredients is extracted from nature and can't be made synthetically, at least not nearly to the same quality - that we don't know how to produce - which is something that happens all the time in recipes.

# VII. Addressing The Fundamental Differences Between One's Conscious Thoughts And Elements Synthesized By Human Beings

One objection that could be brought to this theory of consciousness is to point out that conscious thoughts (e.g. conscious ideas, sounds, images) are very different in some of their basic, fundamental characteristics from the elements synthesized by human beings that emerge within our collective focus (e.g. movies, books, news articles). For example, one's conscious thoughts feel alive and independent from one's individual cells, in

---

[19] For those not familiar with the term, a quick online search will provide a wealth of more detailed definitions.

contrast to anything that seems to arise from human interaction in relation to individual humans.

Another important difference is that one's conscious thoughts give off a sense of first-person unity about one's body and mind. This is best felt in the use of first-person pronouns within the elements that emerge in one's consciousness, such as "I", "my", etc. (e.g. I should do this. This is what I think. I feel good. My skin. My hair.) By contrast, human society is most often referred to using 3$^{rd}$ person appellatives within the elements synthesized by human beings that emerge within our collective focus, when it is referred to as a whole. (example: documentaries/books that discuss human society tend to refer to human society with the impersonal "human society", even though they are elements that may emerge within the collective focus of human beings, where their effect may be understood as "human society reflecting on herself".)

In this chapter, we will address the potential causes for these and other differences in the fundamental characteristics between thoughts synthesized by cells that emerge within one's conscious awareness, and elements synthesized by people that become very popular within human society.

To begin, imagine again how human society looks from the perspective of the alien scientists. See her as an organism growing on the surface of Earth. It would look like an organism, surely, but a multicellular organism? No, a multicellular organism is by definition one whose fundamental structural and functional units are cells. Then what type of organism is human society? Well, if a multi*cellular* organism is an organism whose fundamental structural and functional units are cells, then let us define organisms whose fundamental structural and functional units are multicellular organisms as multizoa[20] organisms.

Let us then look at human society as being a multizoa organism. What can be said about it? Well, the first striking conclusion that presents itself is that human society is a self-emergent multizoa organism, the first of its kind; It does not have any parent. This is in contrast with any multizoa organism similar to human society that may arise in the future, because it would trace its ancestry to human society. For example, if we were to develop the means for interstellar travel, the colonies we would establish on other planets would, from the perspective of the alien scientists, emerge through a process that can be named multizoa reproduction. And the relationship between human society and any multizoa organism that would descend from it would bear much resemblance to the relationship between the first cell that emerged within nature (dubbed by human scientists as the protocell) and all other cells that descended from it through reproduction; Or the relationship between the first multicellular organism, and all other multicellular organisms that were its descendants.

Now, was the very first multicellular organism conscious in the same way that a present-day human is conscious? Of course not. Consciousness evolved over many multicellular generations to get to the level it is today, so we may say that the consciousness of that first multicellular organism - if we are to name it consciousness - would have been primitive in comparison to the consciousness of

---

[20] Zoia is the greek term for "animals."

present day human beings.[21] In conclusion, we may extrapolate that the elements which emerge within the collective focus of human beings inhabiting human society today (books, movies, news articles, etc.) are likely primitive in relation the elements that will emerge within the collective focus of human beings inhabiting any multizoa descendant of human society.

That being said, three factors stand out for why some of the fundamental characteristics present in elements synthesized by one's cells that emerge within their collective focus (conscious human thoughts) differ from the fundamental characteristics of elements synthesized by human beings within human society that emerge within our collective focus:

1. The fact that our human society is a protomultizoa organism, so the elements that presently emerge within the collective focus of human beings inhabiting our human society are most likely primitive in relation to the elements that will emerge within the collective focus of human beings inhabiting the potential multizoa descendants of human society.

2. The fact that human society as a multizoa organism is probably in its very early stages of development, and just like a human child, may not have its consciousness fully formed. (For example, currently only 1\3 of the entire human population has access to the internet, which is a crucial channel of distribution for

---

[21] Based upon the analysis performed in this paper, we could formulate it differently by saying that the elements synthesized by that first multicellular organism's cells which emerged within their collective focus would have been primitive in comparison to the elements synthesized by cells inhabiting present-day human beings which emerge within their collective focus (one's conscious focus).

elements synthesized by human beings whose essence lies in the information they carry.)

3. The different nature of the two types of organisms (multicellular and multizoa) may make certain broad categories of elements exist within the collective focus of a multizoa organism's basic units, but not within the collective focus of a multicellular organism's basic units (one's consciousness) and vice versa. (Example: Neurons do not become celebrities within one's consciousness, because as far as we can tell, they do not have an ego.)

Most likely, it is a combination of these three factors.

As a glimpse into the future however, we may very well imagine documentaries, books, news articles and other types of elements synthesized by human beings that may come to refer to human society in a first person pronoun.[22]

## VIII. Conclusion: How Real-Time Conscious Processes Are Explained

Based upon this explanation of consciousness, every moment within your nervous system, cells and cellular networks are synthesizing various elements (musings, ideas, images, etc.), some of which have the necessary qualities to attract their collective attention and emerge within their collective focus\your conscious awareness, and those are your thoughts right now. And now. And now. When you'll finish reading, you might be thinking about this

---

[22] See Narcis Marincat, *In Principio Res* for a good example of this, as well as a more detailed account of human society as a multizoa organism.

paper, which means that the cells\cellular networks of your nervous system are focusing collectively upon the elements they've synthesized that relates to this paper.

Whatever elements your cells\cellular networks synthesize that do not have the necessary qualities for them to be passed along their "cellular social environment" (by way of neuronal projections) throughout your nervous system do not emerge within your conscious awareness and is part of your subconscious. This is similar to how many of the elements synthesized human beings\human networks do not emerge within our collective focus, because they don't have the necessary qualities for us to pass them along within our social environment as they compete with others. (example: a movie that was not that good, and therefore not that popular.)

We cannot capture a glimpse of these elements "from the outside" as they are passed between individual nervous cells\small cellular networks no matter how powerful our scientific instruments are, because cells exist on a different order of magnitude than human beings - one that is much smaller and much faster in comparison. Our difficulty in comprehending what elements cells transmit between one another is similar to the difficulty the alien scientists would encounter in reading the books and hearing the speech passed between human beings, which would be incredibly problematic no matter the strength of their scientific instruments as well.[23]

---

[23] For a proper treatment of the subject complete with underlying reasoning, see Narcis Marincat (2014) *In Principio Res*, Chapter VIII, #12.

# IX. Conclusion: How The Gap Between Cellular Activity And Consciousness Is Bridged

To conclude, the approach to the nature of thoughts unfolded within these pages bridges the gap between the activity of nervous cells and human consciousness by:

a. Introducing a plausible mechanism through which conscious thoughts are formed by cells\cellular networks: element synthesis.

b. Explaining how these thoughts undergo a process of selection and what this process of selection is: Only those elements cells\cellular networks synthesize that have the necessary qualities to attract their collective attention emerge within one's consciousness; The rest may be considered part of one's subconscious.

c. Revealing that there is a practically impenetrable size and speed barrier between an individual human and an individual cell which makes it virtually impossible for a human to observe the synthesis of thoughts in real time as it is experienced from the perspective of a cell: Human consciousness is essentially made up of elements synthesized by nervous cells that attract their collective focus, which means that the speed of human consciousness is limited by the speed of thought synthesis and propagation; Therefore, human consciousness cannot observe the process of thought synthesis itself, as it is faster than the speed of human thinking; If we add to that the difference in size between a human and a cell, which makes the space within which the process of thought synthesis is taking place infinitesimally small from the perspective of a human, the process of thought synthesis becomes practically invisible from the human perspective, if not for the evidence of its existence in each thought that emerges within one's conscious awareness.

From here, a science of consciousness can be formulated by studying the popular elements within human society and their connection to human beings, and juxtaposing this study with the conscious thoughts, ideas, feelings, sensations emerging within one's conscious awareness, and their connection to individual nervous cells and cellular networks.

# CAN THE NOVEL BIOLOGICAL TRAITS OF MULTICELLULAR ORGANISMS BE CONSIDERED CELLULAR INVENTIONS, IN MUCH THE SAME WAY THAT THE STEAM ENGINE, THE CAR, THE ASTRONOMICAL OBSERVATORY ARE HUMAN INVENTIONS?

Novel traits that emerge within multicellular organisms (the larger brain of mammals, the different physical characteristics of different animals), and that drive the process of macroevolution have been traditionally thought to arise from random mutations in the genetic blueprint of organisms over multicellular generations, even though the exact mechanism by which this happens is not clearly understood.[24] This paper argues that such novel traits are in fact largely the result of contributions brought by cells to the organisms they are part of, contributions which are passed on to the

---

[24] See "A scientific dissent from Darwinism", a continuously growing list of what are now 800 scientists that agree with the statement *"We are skeptical of claims for the ability of random mutation and natural selection to account for the complexity of life. Careful examination of the evidence for Darwinian theory should be encouraged."* http://www.dissentfromdarwin.org

descendants of those organisms, not unlike how the development of skyscrapers, the electric power station, the satellite, the astronomical observatory are the result of contributions brought by human beings to the human society they are part of. Evidence for this thesis will be provided, counterarguments addressed, and then we will proceed to show how this theory bridges molecular changes within the DNA of multicellular organisms with the emergence of novel observable traits within that multicellular organism and its descendants.

# Preface

This work builds upon the thought experiment and related concepts introduced in the sister paper, "CAN CONSCIOUS THOUGHTS BE CONSIDERED 'WORKS OF ART' CREATED BY CELLS, MUCH LIKE HOW MOVIES, BOOKS, VIDEO GAMES ARE WORKS OF ART CREATED BY PEOPLE?" We will continue this preface by quoting from it some of the passages that are most relevant to our present topic, but even so, it is suggested that aforementioned paper be read first.

*"For a long time since microscopes enabled their initial discovery, cells have been generally regarded as no more than simple clog-like machines, or at most, molecular factories.[25]*
*But with continuous improvements in microscope design, in methods of recording cellular activity and in cellular staining*

---

[25] See Edwin W. Taylor, Thomas D. Pollard (Feb 2001) *E.B. Wilson Lecture: The Cell as Molecular Machine* for an example. Retrieved from http://www.ncbi.nlm.nih.gov/pmc/articles/PMC30940/

*techniques, there has been increasing consensus starting with the end of the 20*<sup>*th*</sup> *century that rather then being mindless drones, cells (we are placing an emphasis on nervous cells in this paper) are in fact unique, independent, oftentimes unpredictable entities. Modern evidence in support of this theory can be found in our present understanding of just how varied and complex cellular means of communication are*[26]*, the vast amount of new nervous cell types that are being discovered*[27]*, the ever increasing pallet of factors that we learn are influencing cellular actions*[28]*, etc. (For more on this, you may visit Jon Lieff's excellent blog on the subject.*[29]*)*

*Cells are much smaller than humans. Cells move much faster than humans as well (again, we are placing an emphasis on nervous cells, which are known to be able to send upwards of a hundred nervous impulses every second) - but that's true only when interpreting things from our human perspective. It doesn't mean that cells are small, or that they move very fast from the perspective of a cell - indeed, given the fact that cellular action & communication has to be very precise despite the microscopic area in which they unfold and their impressive speed by human standards, evidence points to the contrary. There will be more said on the matter of temporal relativity throughout the paper, but for the sake of the argument,*

---

[26] Jon Lieff (September 21, 2014 )*The Remarkable Language of Cells*. Retrieved from http://jonlieffmd.com/ blog/the-remarkable-language-of-cells

[27] Jon Lieff (October 12, 2014 ) *How Many Different Kinds of Neurons Are There*. Retrieved from http://jonlieffmd.com/blog/how-many-different-kinds-of-neurons-are-there

[28] Jon Lieff (October 19, 2014 ) *Does Activity Determine Synaptic Creation and Pruning* Retrieved from http://jonlieffmd.com/blog/does-activity-determine-synaptic-creation-and-pruning

[29] http://jonlieffmd.com/

entertain this assumption from this point: That a day passing from the perspective of a human being can equal to a year's passing from the perspective of a cell. (Again, emphasis on nervous cells.)"

"...Based upon the points made thus far, we may entertain the possibility that **a human's conscious focus is essentially comprised of the elements synthesized by that human's nervous cells and networks of nervous cells that have the necessary qualities to attract their collective attention** (e.g. particular ideas, feelings, sensations, etc.), **and that this conscious focus is not unlike the collective attention of human beings within human society**, which is essentially comprised of elements synthesized by human beings and human networks (e.g. songs, books, movies, videos of cats playing the piano...basically, any element that has its essence in the information it carries, rather than its physical basis) that have the necessary qualities to become very popular within human society. This is the together-knowing theory of consciousness.
Note: 'Collective attention' may sometimes be referred to as 'collective focus' (as in 'collective focus of cells and cellular networks', or 'collective focus of human beings'). The two terms may be used interchangeably."

"...But are we able to offer further evidence in favor of this hypothesis? To address this question, entertain the following thought experiment:
    Imagine that a group of very large extraterrestrials (each one roughly the size of Earth), and also very slow (for whom a human year would be the equivalent to the timespan of merely a day) have their spaceship discover a "strange fluorescence" emanating from Earth's surface as they peruse the galaxies. As a consequence, large

*as they are, they approach the vicinity of Earth, and discover human society growing on it. Also imagine that it's the first time they encounter anything remotely resembling human society in their entire history of space explorations. They are in fact extremely different beings from us. In their situation, how would they define human society? From their perspective (so large and so...slow) they would see human society as a whole - as kind of a moss-like organism streaked along Earth's surface (not unlike how a human being sees the human body as a unified whole, even though we know it to be made up of cells.) Despite the fact that they would be looking at human society, these extraterrestrials wouldn't be able to perceive individual humans at first, because for them, human beings would be of a microscopic size.*

*Let's imagine however that these are science prone lifeforms, so they use microscopes, endoscopes and so on to analyze this "being" growing on Earth's surface down to its "microscopic"' structure...and they discover the existence of humans. Following a healthy degree of observation, would they not proclaim us in the end the fundamental structural and functional units of human society, responsible for such things as human society's metabolic function, the growth of its body, etc., just like how we've defined the cell as the fundamental structural and functional unit of the human body? From their perspective, they probably would.*

*But at the same time, would these humongous and slow aliens not have a very simplistic view of humans, due to extremely limited information they (and their instruments) can pick up from complex human action because of the difference in size and speed between them and us? For example, they wouldn't be able to decode human speech; A person holding a one hour monologue would be compressed in time for the alien scientists to an instant...to a "sound impulse" at most, if their instruments would be equipped with the ability to pick up human speech at all. This is much like how we interpret electrical/electrochemical interactions taking place between nervous cells as "nervous impulses", rather than cellular speech, or anything as complex as that. In other words, the perspective of the alien scientists is becoming very similar to our human perspective of cells."*

*"...To illustrate the potency of the analogy between* the alien scientists' relationship to a human *and* a human's relationship to a cell, *imagine that the alien scientists decide to send an asteroid towards Earth, though from a safe distance to emulate a natural occurrence, and just stand back to observe the results. And let's say that our astronomers observe it in safe time, and that we eventually decide to send a missile to obliterate the incoming asteroid. Would the alien scientists from their perspective not interpret the sending of the missile as* **the action of human society**, *rather than the result of countless human beings that were involved in such a defense response? And isn't this much like how we interpret catching a ball during a play of catch as the action of the human being playing, even though we know that the person's body is in fact made up of countless cells, which are acting in concert to catch the ball? It is just natural from the human size and speed to interpret things that way in the latter case, in the same way that it is natural from the size and speed of the alien scientists to interpret the sending of the missile as the action of human society.* [30]*..."*

---

[30] A more in depth account of the alien scientists thought experiment and its many uses, as well an explanation as to why it is such a potent analogy to a

*"...Imagine again how human society looks from the perspective of the alien scientists. See her as an organism growing on the surface of Earth. It would look like an organism, surely, but a multicellular organism? No, a multicellular organism is by definition one whose fundamental structural and functional units are cells. Then what type of organism is human society? Well, if a multicellular organism is an organism whose fundamental structural and functional units are cells, then let us define organisms whose fundamental structural and functional units are multicellular organisms as* **multizoa[31] organisms.**

*Let us then look at human society as being a multizoa organism. What can be said about it? Well, the first striking thing that presents itself is that human society is a self-emergent multizoa organism, the first of its kind; It does not have any parent. This is in contrast with any multizoa organism similar to human society that may arise in the future, because it would trace its ancestry to human society. For example, if we were to develop the means for interstellar travel, the colonies we would establish on other planets would, from the perspective of the alien scientists, emerge through a process that can be named multizoa reproduction. And the relationship between human society and any multizoa organism that would descend from it would bear much resemblance to the relationship between the first cell that emerged within nature (dubbed by human scientists as the protocell) and all other cells that descended from it through reproduction; Or the relationship*

---

human's relationship with a cell can be found in the book *In Principio Res* by Narcis Marincat, from which this paper draws its inspiration.

[31] Zoia is the greek term for "animals."

*between the first multicellular organism, and all other multicellular organisms that were its descendants.*

*Now, was the very first multicellular organism conscious in the same way that a present-day human is conscious? Of course not. Consciousness evolved over many multicellular generations to get to the level it is today, so we may say that the consciousness of that first multicellular organism - if we are to name it consciousness - would have been primitive in comparison to the consciousness of present day human beings. In conclusion, we may extrapolate that the elements which emerge within the collective focus of human beings inhabiting human society today (books, movies, news articles, etc.) are likely primitive in relation the elements that will emerge within the collective focus of human beings inhabiting any multizoa descendant of human society."*

Again, if you have not, it is strongly recommended that you read the initial paper in this series before continuing so as to get a proper account of the concepts used henceforth. The quotes presented in this preface essentially serve as a helpful reminder for those who read it, and as a teaser for those who haven't.

# I. Introduction

We will begin this paper's introduction by outlining the main premises underscoring modern evolutionary theory:

1. There is a variation in the biological traits displayed by the individuals that make up a population of organisms: For example, some giraffes have a longer neck than others.
2. There is differential reproduction. Since the environment can't support unlimited population growth, not all individuals get to reproduce to their full potential. For example, giraffes with longer necks could have better reached tree leaves and survive to reproduce more often than giraffes with shorter necks.
3. There is heredity – Traits get passed on from one generation of organisms to another. In our example, the long neck trait has a genetic basis, so it gets passed from one giraffe to its descendant.
4. The more advantageous trait - long necks - which allows giraffes to have more offspring, becomes more common in the population, because the individuals carrying that trait will have more chances to survive and reproduce.
5. The main mechanism for the emergence of novel traits within an organism is the random mutations that take place in the genome of that organism, which is has been named the main driving force behind evolutionary processes.

In other words, whenever there is variation, differential reproduction, and heredity, evolution by natural selection will arise as an outcome, and random mutations are the main driving force of variation in cellular organisms.

That being said, we shall continue the alien scientists thought experiment from where we left off in the initial paper:

Imagine that, after performing a number of scientific experiments on our human society, the alien scientists eventually left this galactic area satisfied with the data they've collected. Their species did not come back to our corner of the universe for a few billion years, after which time they remembered human society and decided to see what changed since their kind first ventured here, and what they discovered upon returning simply astonished them. The long-past first expedition that their ancestors went on years ago (billions of years from the perspective of human beings) documented the existence of only one multizoa organism: Our human society. But now, upon returning, they were surprised to witness the existence of a large number and variety of multizoa organisms, displaying strikingly different structural differences (i.e. what the alien scientists would consider multizoa traits) and behaviors between them. Some of these multizoa organisms were indeed rooted to the surface of planets and somewhat resembled the description of our human society, whereas others had motile, agile bodies and engaged in complex activities - what we would consider to be human-built starships.

With the help of their advanced scientific instruments, the alien scientists discovered stationary as well as motile multizoa organisms that lived underwater on various planets as well.

This large number and diversity of multizoa life had not been noted by the initial expedition at all, though a great part of that expedition took place in this part of the universe. Quite naturally, the alien scientists wondered how this was possible, and as it tends to be with the initial stages in the life of a great discovery, a number of competing hypotheses began to appear.

# II. Speculations, Gathering Evidence And The Final Theory

One explanation that the alien scientists came up with for why the first expedition did not note the existence of such numbers and diversity of multizoa organisms was that their ancestors somehow overlooked the multizoa life they now had before them, but to most of them this scenario seemed unfathomable. The cruder object detection systems their ships had back then might have missed small signs of life, such as the existence of multizoa organisms similar in kind to our human society disparately placed within neighboring galaxies, but they would have surely captured any one motile organism (starship) moving in their vicinity, not to say anything about the bustling activity the alien scientists were currently witnessing. And in any case, it wouldn't explain the real origin of this multizoa profusion of numbers and diversity.

Others had theorized that perhaps the ancestors of present multizoa organisms came into being spontaneously during the time that passed after the initial expedition, which fitted with their conclusion that our current human society "had no apparent parent", reached after the alien scientists which discovered it performed extensive research on the subject. This hypothesis was called spontaneous generation, and it initially attracted a number of influential supporters.[32]

---

[32] The theory of spontaneous generation in respect to cells dominated the human scientific field up until the 19th century – until then, it was generally thought that cells and some multicellular organisms came into being spontaneously. Reference: James E. Strick (2003) Sparks of Life: Darwinism and the Victorian Debates over Spontaneous Generation.

Another explanation was that all of these new multizoa organisms were descendants of the one described by their ancestors, and/or of similar organisms which, unbeknownst to them, were living within neighboring galaxies at that time, but unfortunately, they had no satisfying way of explaining how reproduction could have led to such multizoa diversity – not initially. And, with no defining evidence to point in one direction or another, you can imagine that the debates among them were constant and ongoing.

In the meantime, diligent as they were, the alien scientists began to classify multizoa organism into taxonomic groups (like species, kingdom, class) and engaged in long-term observations to get a detailed understanding of their life-cycle. Such research yielded a number of interesting findings. For example, all the multizoa organisms they witnessed being born emerged from other multizoa organisms by way of their reproduction, yet they saw no evidence of spontaneous generation taking place.

They also saw that there is a variation in the traits displayed by the members of any one multizoa species – for example, within motile multizoa species (i.e. multizoa species whose members are starships), they noted differences in the sensitivity of motile multizoa organism's sense organs (what we would deem as its observatories and antennae), in the shape and freedom of motion of appendages, in the shape of the hull – and such differences surfaced between the members of every multizoa species that they documented.

But before long, they also found that some multizoa species closely resemble one another, and that they are made separate only by slight differences that lead them to be classified as different species. For example, the only fundamental difference between the members of two motile multizoa species may be an extra appendage in one of them.

   These findings began to trace for the alien scientists the contour of a mechanism that would explain how the diversity of multizoa life emerged, for it led them to consider the possibility that, just like there are variations in the same traits between the members of a multizoa species, sometimes completely new traits can emerge within one member of a particular species, making the species branch out into novel species. And speculations among them arose that if that trait confers an advantage in the organisms' ability to reproduce and survive, that member will most likely produce offspring and the species will grow in number, becoming an established species within its environment. The extra appendage could have very well been such a novel trait. Then, the same process can take place within this new species, and so on...and this accumulation of novel traits would lead in time to the development of multizoa species that are vastly different from one another. On the other hand, if the novel trait is disadvantageous to the organism's ability to survive or reproduce, the new species is likely to soon die off; And some traits could offer no evolutionary advantage or disadvantage at all, making them benign, with little to no influence on their own. In fact, some alien scientists speculated that there may be important differences in traits between the members of the same multizoa species that they haven't noted because they aren't apparent.

* At around the same time, their scrupulous scientific investigations also began to reveal fossilized multizoa organisms at a few sites sparingly placed throughout the galactic area, and some of the well-preserved fossils bore little to no resemblance to the multizoa species currently documented to exist, which provided evidence for

the existence of other multizoa species which had gone extinct, lending support to the theory they were developing.

But what exactly drove the emergence of novel multizoa traits? With no means to perceive the information being passed between individual human beings due to the difference in size-speed, with the simplistic account of humans that is a product of such difference, and in light of the findings derived from their observations and experiments, the alien scientists reached the conclusion that such traits are the result of random mutations which normally occur while the organism comes into being before birth, or within the initial stages of a multizoa organism's existence as the organism is still growing, just like variations between the same traits do.

Later, as more multizoa fossils were uncovered, they saw that the simplest fossilized multizoa organisms are those which tended to be the oldest, with more complex species appearing later, and that the youngest fossils are those which, on average, most closely resemble the current living species of multizoa organism. They also began to notice that the different species of multizoa organisms, living and fossilized seemed to fall into a natural order based on shared common traits – which looked a lot like a multizoa tree of life.

After careful study of these and other related findings acquired through painstaking research, the alien scientists formulated what became a widely accepted scientific theory within their circles: Evolution through the natural selection of multizoa organisms that underwent random mutations.

# III. Evolution Through The Natural Selection Of Multizoa Organisms That Underwent Random Mutations

The theory goes as follows: Multizoa life evolved gradually from a single multizoa species that lived billions of years ago (and perhaps our current human society was part of that species), which over time branched off into numerous new and diverse multizoa species through the process of the natural selection of multizoa organisms that underwent random mutations, which is the main driving force behind the evolutionary process.

The theory of natural selection is relatively simple to understand: It states that if the members within a multizoa species display a variation in traits, if those traits are heritable and if they have an effect upon the organism's ability to survive and reproduce, then the individuals within a multizoa species which acquire traits that offer an advantage upon its ability to survive and reproduce will be most likely to do so – will be naturally selected - and so, those traits will either spread through the population of that multizoa species, while detrimental traits are weeded off, leading over time for a species to become better adapted to its environment; or, if the trait makes the organism sufficiently different from its peers, it will lead to the establishment of a different multizoa species altogether.

As noted earlier, the alien scientists posited that new multizoa traits emerge by means of random mutations undertaken by members within the various species of multizoa organism.

# IV. Juxtaposition Of Theories

Should you not be aware of the resemblance, the theory outlined in the former chapter in respect to multizoa organisms is more or less what the theory of evolution through the natural selection of random mutations that human beings have used to explain the development of multicellular organisms postulates as well. At the same time, the evidence given within these pages in support for the theory in respect to multizoa organisms is the equivalent of evidence often cited in support of the modern theory of evolution in respect to multicellular organisms (e.g. fossil records, variation in traits, the nested hierarchy implicit in building a phylogenetic tree).

Nevertheless, you might feel the need to shed some light on this theory when applied to human societies and let the alien scientists know that there are no random developments when it comes to the human world – "We're not like the cells which make up the human body, we're rational beings! It is our intellect and diligence that lead to beneficial changes in the societies we establish." If we knew the conclusions they derived from all their other experiments and findings, there may be a number of other corrections we would want to make, but one should take into account their position: The alien scientists are searching for a logical understanding of things without possessing knowledge of our complex ways of communication or what this communication transmits – due to the difference in size-speed, the words we utter, which concern a world that is very different from their own, vanish in the flash of an instant for them, as do other actions we perform second by second. We know that what they perceive as "random mutations", like new social structures, means of transportation or communication techniques are the end-result of a process that implicates the willful actions of a great number of people (pieced together sometimes by chance, sometimes through human planning, oftentimes through a combination of the two). In the case of the internet for example some helped build the computer, while others came up with the world wide web protocols, others with optical cables, and so on, but the inquisitive aliens would have no way of seeing these parallel occurrences converging with purpose to produce a multizoa trait – indeed, even we may find it demanding to follow their intricate progression (which is why there are books written on the history of the internet, and contentious points between them around certain crucial points in that history).

It is true, the theory of evolution through natural selection can be applied to the future evolution of multizoa organisms as readily as it presently applies to multicellular organisms:

1. There is a variation in traits: For example, some multizoa organisms have long appendages, some have shorter ones.
2. There is heredity – Traits get passed on from one multizoa generation to another. (Much like how we build houses to be roughly the same with one another even though we theoretically have the possibility to build each one differently, more efficiently than the last, upon reaching a certain degree of complexity, it is likely that we would build the descendant of a multizoa organisms very similarly with its parent as well.[33])
3. There is differential reproduction – Some members of a multizoa species may reproduce at a faster rate or more than others, sometimes due to their trait differences. For example, if

---

[33] For a detailed explanation, see Narcis Marincat (2014) *In Principio Res*, chapter II, #5.

an unpredictable catastrophe like an asteroid shower were to suddenly rain down upon an area of the galaxy inhabited by a multizoa species, the individuals which have traits that would allow them to effectively defend themselves (like starships with a reinforced hull) would be most likely to survive, while the others would have less of a chance, and those traits which allowed them to live would be passed on to their offspring.

4. A trait which allows the multizoa organism to have more offspring or that makes it better adapted within its environment is likely to become more common in the multizoa population of which the organism is part of. (See point 3 for an example)

But how do the traits that undergo natural selection emerge in the first place? Due to the impenetrable size-speed barrier, to the alien scientists the appearance of a particular multizoa trait would be indistinguishable from a chance occurrence, from randomness, whereas from the vantage point of human beings, they are recognized as the product of human imagination, human creation, human determination, human cooperation, human design. The point of view taken by our larger brethren is to be understood, as the alien scientists would not have access to the world of a human from their vantage point, and thus they would be unable to grasp the unique existence of each human being, nor what drove them second by second, minute by minute to provide the individual contributions which lead to this or that "trait", or how a novel multizoa trait was encoded to potentially manifest itself in a future human settlement established on a different planet, or a future starship. This lack of information might lead the alien scientists to develop a mechanistic understanding of multizoa organisms, and their evolution.

   Yet, by acknowledging the validity of this thought experiment, we might come to place under question the present scientific explanation for the way in which newly evolved traits emerge within multicellular organisms: random mutations. From the vantage point of human beings, the emergence of novel traits displayed by cellular societies may be indistinguishable from the product of chance occurrences. But from the vantage point of a cell, such traits may come to be perceived as partly or fully the product of cellular imagination, cellular creation, cellular determination, cellular cooperation, cellular design. Perhaps the point of view endorsed by human scientists thus far is to be understood, as they have little access to the cellular world as it is naturally experienced by cells, and thus have a hard time grasping or following the unique existence of these beings, what drives them instant by instant, second by second to provide the individual contributions which lead the emergence of such traits, or, without acknowledging the size-speed parallax (i.e. the possibility to look at the world from different size-speeds and derive very different information from it as a consequence), recognize that such contributions can manifest themselves beyond the human gaze. [34]

---

[34] Humans are one step ahead of the alien scientists by being able to correlate differences in traits between different species of multicellular organisms with genetic and epigenetic changes in DNA. However, the anthropocentric view of time has led to the postulation that the main mechanism behind genetic changes in DNA, and therefore behind emerging multicellular traits are caused by random genetic mutations that arise while the cell is replicating, although the correlation between DNA and traits could also point to the existence of an as of yet unknown method by which a cell can encode information within its DNA to document an emerging trait within its society. But due to the size-speed barrier between humans and cells, no encoding of such a mutation has been documented in real-

In other words, it is likely that the multicellular mutations naturally selected during the evolution of multicellular organisms are purposeful mutations developed by the cells that live\have lived within these organisms, despite the general present perspective of human scientists that they are they outcome of randomness, just as the multizoa mutations that would be naturally selected during the evolution of multizoa organisms would be purposeful mutations developed by the people who would inhabit these organisms, despite the conclusion of the alien scientists that they are random. The perspective of human beings and of the alien scientists that these mutations are random is just the natural effect of the size-speed barrier between them and the beings they are studying.

Now, let us also employ some common sense. If one were to be transported across space and time to a far off descendant of our current human society growing upon another planet and find that instead of skyscrapers, there are buildings built of living biological material, and instead of cars running on fossil fuels, there are flying automobiles running on hydrogen or solar power, and wherever there would be the need for repetitive labor one would find complex automatons doing the job instead of human beings, one would not be able to envision any random process that could have possibly produced such changes gradually over time over generations of multizoa organisms, so how can one accept this view in respect to the evolution of multicellular organisms and the development of their novel traits, which are themselves oftentimes incredibly complex?

---

time, and therefore the current scientific framework is understandable: Current scientific knowledge seems to allow for the theory of unguided mutations. The ideas discussed here may however provide a logical basis for tipping the balance between these theories.

That being said, it is important to take note that even if the development of novel biological traits are not random occurrences, but are purposefully achieved by the basic units of organisms, the process of natural selection still plays an important role in the development of both multicellular as well as multizoa organisms. To better understand why, let us engage in another thought experiment:

Say that our current human society were to reproduce on 100 different planets, each implementing different, but theoretically feasible and promising changes in the way it is governed, the way it is structured, and so on. (To offer some examples, imagine the difference between capitalism, communism and anarchy; or the difference between futuristic cities based on sustainable principles, with self-sustaining homes that do not depend on any centralized grid to offer food, water, shelter, warmth, and conventional cities of the type we see around us today within our own human society.) From the perspective of the alien scientists, such design derivations would translate into different multizoa traits. Now, although the changes in design within each multizoa organism would be done with the best of intentions by the human beings who inhabit them, due to the complex factors that are come into play within the development of such an organism, it might not always produce a favorable outcome. But, of course, evolution cannot take place without assuming a certain amount of risk that comes with taking an untrodden path. Therefore, while some members of this hundred batch would emerge as especially promising, the design derivations implemented in other multizoa organisms that are part of the same hundred might lead to unpredictable, unfavorable results that would have a detrimental effect to their fitness, their ability to healthily mature, survive and reproduce. And of course, those multizoa organisms that emerge as promising would be more likely to grow in numbers within their environment – in other words, they would likely be those "naturally selected" to perpetuate their "species". And that is how natural selection would still play a role in the case of teleological mutations. This thought experiment can be played out in respect with multicellular organisms as well, with the same result.

So, to summarize this theory in a language that applies to both multicellular and multizoa organisms, the evolution of organisms takes place through the natural selection of organisms that undergo teleological mutations developed by their basic units. Teleological in this case just means purposeful mutations developed by the basic units of these organisms - cells in the case of multicellular organisms, human beings in the case of multizoa organisms. However, would the development of the teleological mutations leading to novel multizoa traits be unpredictable? Highly likely, at least for the most part! No one would have predicted the development of the internet as it is today a mere century ago for example, not humans and certainly not the alien scientists, as the conflation of countless human minds, human creations, human endeavors, human designs which lead to it produced unpredictable outcomes. Unpredictable, yes, but not random.

So, to put this as well in a language that applies both to multicellular and multizoa organisms, the development of a novel trait within an organism can be unpredictable, yes, but that doesn't mean that it's random.

# V. Counterarguments: The Unpredictable Outcome Of Sexual Reproduction

One of the counterarguments that can be brought to the theory of multicellular evolution by way of natural selection of organisms that underwent teleological mutations has to do with the fact that animals reproduce sexually. As you may know, sexual reproduction is a process that creates a new organism by combining the genetic information of the two parent organisms. Sexual reproduction begins with production of sex cells via meiosis (a process that halves the genetic code of the organism as its sex cell is made in preparation for combination with another sex cell). During meiosis, two processes that are generally considered to be random take place: one is the pairing of homologous chromosomes, in which one member of the pairs of similar chromosomes within the genetic material (each pair has one chromosome from the maternal side and one from the paternal side, called homologous chromosomes) is randomly swapped for the formation of a sex cells. Second is the process of homologous recombination, in which essentially the DNA sequences of the organism are randomly swapped between homologous chromosomes before splitting in half, thus producing new combinations of genes for each chromosome. These two processes are jointly known as genetic recombination.[35]

---

[35] Though evidence has surfaced that genetic recombination is not an entirely random process. See Brick et. al. (2012) Genetic recombination is directed away from functional genomic elements in mice for an example.

The seemingly random nature of genetic recombination[36], combined with the fact that it is not known which sex cells are actually fertilized and manage to create an organism makes the process of selecting which traits actually get passed on to offspring during sexual reproduction appear very much like a game of chance.

So, the specific counterargument to the theory of evolution of multicellular organisms through the natural selection of organisms that underwent teleological mutations could be formulated as follows: Why would cells go through all the trouble of encoding the novel developments within the society of cells they are part of, only to have such a seemingly "random" process as sexual reproduction decide if the genetic information that encodes such developments will be transmitted to the next generation?

Before beginning to address this issue, it is worth noting that sexual reproduction stands as one of the greatest mysteries in biology, with a long history of having both its use and its origins hotly debated. To this day, there are contentious points regarding both when and why sexual reproduction arose[37], or how random the process of genetic recombination really is. (see footnote 35)

That being said, the reproduction mechanism of multizoa organisms that may foreseeably arise within human society would likely be quite different in nature from that of multicellular organisms in general, true. Two points may be made to address this difference:

---

[36] Encyclopaedia Britannica, Recombination. Retrieved from http://www.britannica.com/EBchecked/topic/493676/recombination
[37] Goodenough & Heitman (2014) Origins of Eukaryotic Sexual Reproduction

1. The first-generation multicellular organisms would have probably had to reproduce asexually[38] - a reproduction mechanism that shares a closer relationship with the one that our present human society is likely to develop - for it would not have had partners with which to reproduce sexually.

2. Who knows how multizoa reproduction would evolve in the course of a few multizoa generations? Perhaps at times, it may come to involve cooperation between a pair or number of multizoa organisms, for it would be found that bringing together the insight and knowledge from different multizoa organisms would increase the fitness of the new starship\planetary colony. And how would the "multizoa traits" that get passed from one generation to the next be selected from each organisms?

First, in order for such "multizoa sexual reproduction" to occur, the process of multizoa reproduction would likely have to be standardized, so that information may be put together from all these different multizoa organisms.

Would that mean the prior development of a multizoa "genetic code" - that is, a standardized way in which each multizoa organism would record and store the basic information about its structure, with sections that would be swappable between multizoa organisms that employ the same standardized way? Say, for example, that during "sexual multizoa reproduction", one of the parent-multizoa organisms would have better, more efficient house designs than another, so it would be agreed upon that the "housing section" of the multizoa "genetic code" would be copied to the "genetic code" of the newly forming multizoa organism, making it

---

[38] Simply put, a reproduction mechanism through which offspring arise from the genetic material of a single parent organism, and thus the offspring shares the traits of that parent organism alone.

the official way in which the members of that nascent multizoa organism build houses. Of course, the process of building houses could evolve within that descendent-multizoa organism as it grows, so at a later time, its "genetic code" could be updated to fit the current way in which houses are built within it.

But perhaps for more "trivial" aspects of the multizoa organism's "genetic information" - or in cases where the traits of multizoa parents are markedly similar - there would be some sort of random draw over which trait actually gets selected - say, in the way food is stored.

What the speculations in point two aim to show is that there's a possibility that multizoa organisms will come to reproduce themselves "sexually" over time, and in certain conditions (due to the perceived use of such a reproduction technique) and that at least to a certain extent, randomness could play a role in the recombination of multizoa "genetic information" during the reproduction process...A process that, if observed by the alien scientists, would probably seem completely random even though it would be driven by precise human considerations and might be as puzzling to the extraterrestrials as multicellular sexual reproduction is for human scientists.

# VI. The Cambrian Explosion Explained

An interesting result derived from looking at the evolution of biological systems through the lens polished in this paper is that it seems to solve the mystery of the Cambrian explosion.

The Cambrian explosion is an important event in the evolution of multicellular organisms that human scientists estimate started around 540 million years ago.[39] Up until that time, the fossil record shows that most organisms on Earth were simple, comprised mainly of unicellular organisms occasionally organized into colonies. But during the next 60 million years, almost all animal phyla appeared, with as many as 2/3 of them appearing in approximately the first 20 million years of this period. (animal phyla are the basic body forms that animals found throughout nature display, like the chordata, which includes the human body form and that of other vertebrates, the antropoda, which includes arachnids like spiders, or the mollusca, which, unsurprisingly, includes the mollusks). This 20 million year period or rapid multicellular development is called the Cambrian explosion, and because the theory of evolution through the natural selection of organisms that underwent random mutations does not explain the reason for why such a flurrying emergence of multicellular diversity would have taken place after the initial development of multicellular life, this explosion has been puzzling human scientists ever since the fossil record enabled its discovery.

But the theory of evolution through the natural selection of organisms that undergo teleological mutations can provide an explanation, albeit indirectly.

We've already stated how, if human society were to develop the ability to reproduce, human beings could easily envision implementing design derivations within human society's multizoa descendants that would differentiate them from their parent. From the perspective of the alien scientists, these design derivations would translate into novel multizoa traits.

---

[39] P V Sukumaran (2004) Cambrian Explosion of Life: the Big Bang in Metazoan Evolution

If everything goes right and they are healthy, the descendants of human society would probably have a much easier time reproducing then our human society, as they would inherit the blueprint for the multizoa bodily systems that would allow them to do so from their parent, so these bodily systems would be able to mature much faster during their development.

Human beings that would live within these newly born multizoa organisms would most likely pursue new avenues of multizoa design while reproducing, giving birth to multizoa organism with novel traits, that if successful, would go on reproducing, and the same could apply for the next generations. (During this period, there may be human beings that arise in the field of multizoa design whose contributions to the field would set the standard, much as it happens with every human field). All of this would translate into multizoa organisms branching off into new species, and this may be recorded in the multizoa fossil record that the alien scientists are analyzing as a rapid diversification of multizoa life.

As a consequence, the starships observed by the alien scientists visiting this part of the universe after so long would likely be the culmination of human beings forming societies for eons, very well adapted to their environment, and their bodies would have a marked degree of complexity, with its various bodily systems being highly integrated with one another. What this complexity means however, is that if a fundamental structural change in their design were to be implemented in one of their bodily systems even with the best of intentions, like say the way they "digest" resources from their environment, it is quite possible for that design derivation to cascade into adjacent systems in an unpredictable manner to the detriment of their optimum function, like for example in their individual central processing units. So, as long as the environment in which these multizoa species live - to which their bodies are so well adapted - would not experience dramatic changes, the risk of implementing new fundamental derivations in their design would outweigh the potential benefits. Applying the same principle to all the other multizoa species that are very well adapted to their environment and have complex bodily systems, what the multizoa fossil record would likely show overall is a flurrying emergence of novel multizoa types following the development of the protomultizoa organism's ability to reproduce, and as teleological mutations developed generation after generation of multizoa organisms lead the protoorganism's descendants to be more efficiently adapted to their environment and more complex, the diversification of multizoa types would tone down. That initial period of flurrying emergence would contrast with the ensuing period of relatively small macroscopic multizoa changes in the fossil record, which would give the former an "explosive" character that would no doubt puzzle the alien scientists if they would try to understand it through the lens of multizoa evolution by way of the natural selection of multizoa organisms that underwent random mutations, much like the correlating puzzlement experienced by human scientists in regard to the Cambrian explosion.

But, as we've seen, by replacing randomness with teleology - that is, through the theory of evolution by way of the natural selection of organisms that underwent teleological mutations (the possible unpredictability of the final result of such mutations notwithstanding) - one can provide a sensible explanation.

So to summarize in a language that applies to both organisms of interest, the theory of evolution through the natural selection of organisms that undergo teleological mutations predicts that many new design derivations of a protoorganism would emerge in its descendants following the development of bodily systems which provide it with the ability to reproduce, and as their design derivations would become more and more efficient in their environment and more complex over generations, their basic structure (or bodily forms) would acquire more and more stability, a theory which is in line with the Cambrian explosion, and also foresees a correlating multizoa event following the development of human society's ability to reproduce.

# VII. Conclusion - The Evolution Of Organisms Through The Natural Selection Of Individuals That Underwent Favorable Teleological Mutations

Let us briefly outline the approach to evolution that this paper introduces, and the main steps taken to reach it:

We saw how, from the vantage point of the alien scientists, novel traits displayed by multizoa organisms could be perceived as the outcome of random mutations, due to the fact that they do not have informational access to the human world because of the size-speed barrier between our world and theirs. We also know that from the human vantage point, these multizoa mutations (present day examples include the development of sky-scrapers, of concrete roads, etc.) are not perceived to be random at all; rather, they can be seen as the products of countless human minds, human creations, human endeavors, and so, they are teleological – they are purposeful.

Similarly, human beings describe the development of novel traits displayed by multicellular organisms as the product of random mutations. But we know that there is a difference in the size and speed between humans and cells similar to the difference in size-speed between the alien scientists and humans, and if the alien scientists are unable to understand the logic behind choices made by humans moment by moment in their natural, normal setting that would lead to the emergence of a novel multizoa trait in large part because of this difference, then we might be unable to do so as well in respect to individual cells. Therefore, we may argue that these random cellular mutations are not random at all, that rather they are teleological mutations whose development we cannot follow from our size-speed due to the barrier imposed by the difference in space-time between our world and the world of a cell. [40]

However, that does not mean that such mutations are entirely preplanned. Much like how the invention of the printing press or the computer was generally unpredictable, and oftentimes involved taking advantage of chance occurrences happening within human society by blending them with purpose, the mutations that lead to the evolution of multicellular organisms can be unpredictable, and may involve cells and cellular networks taking advantage of chance occurrences happening within a multicellular organism by blending them with purpose.

Also, the fact that mutations are teleological does not mean that natural selection does not play a role in their development. Indeed, even done with the best of intentions by its basic units, the implementation of novel traits within an organism may lead to

---

[40] Except for the general idea that they somehow correlate with genetic and epigenetic changes in DNA.

unpredictable, unfavorable changes to the detriment of the organism's ability to survive and thrive within its environment, and the organisms that come to emerge successful, that are well adapted to their environment are those that are "naturally selected" to perpetuate their species. However, what gets naturally selected changes, for rather than being organisms that acquire novel traits through random mutations, it is the natural selection of organisms that underwent teleological mutations.

Looking at the evolution of multicellular organisms in this light, a number of mysteries in this field seem to be explained, such as:

a. How novel traits are encoded within the DNA of organisms - Rather than being random, it is done by cells, who from their size-speed know how to achieve this.
b. Why the Cambrian explosion took place - it is similar to the explosion in the diversity of multizoa organisms that would take place once human society achieves the ability to reproduce.

# A NOVEL APPROACH TO MORALITY: DO UNTO YOUR NEIGHBOR AS YOU WOULD HAVE THE CELLS OF YOUR BODY DO UNTO THEIR NEIGHBORING CELLS

The most often espoused secular notion of morality today, in light of the latest findings about human society's place in the universe is that of moral relativism, taken here to mean that what may be morally permissible to you may not be morally permissive for me based on our beliefs. That is, morality is relative to the observer. Analyzed coldly and logically, this view invariably leads to the conclusion that one can and should do whatever one chooses, as long as one does not get caught (at least in the case of morally questionable acts.) Though a conclusion rarely stated out loud, it is one that is often applied.

This paper will draw upon the end-points of the first of the three papers in this series to give a new approach to morality, one which, although entirely secular and materialistic, stands in contrast with that of moral relativism. The moniker of this novel approach to morality is "Do unto your neighbor as you would have the cells of your body do unto their neighboring cells."

# Preface

This work builds upon the thought experiment and related concepts introduced in the first of its two sister papers, "CAN CONSCIOUS THOUGHTS BE CONSIDERED 'WORKS OF ART' CREATED BY CELLS, MUCH LIKE HOW MOVIES, BOOKS, VIDEO GAMES ARE WORKS OF ART CREATED BY PEOPLE?" and "CAN NOVEL BIOLOGICAL TRAITS OF MULTICELLULAR ORGANISMS BE CONSIDERED CELLULAR INVENTIONS, MUCH LIKE HOW THE STEAM ENGINE, THE CAR, THE ASTRONOMICAL OBSERVATORY ARE HUMAN INVENTIONS?" We will therefore continue this preface by quoting from the first paper some of the passages that are most relevant to our present topic, but even so, it is suggested that both aforementioned papers be read first (click on their individual titles to read them in your browser) so that a firm grasp of the general approach taken by this paper is achieved.

*"For a long time since microscopes enabled their initial discovery, cells have been generally regarded as no more than simple clog-like machines, or at most, molecular factories.[41]*

*But with continuous improvements in microscope design, in methods of recording cellular activity and in cellular staining techniques, there has been increasing consensus starting with the end of the 20<sup>th</sup> century that rather then being mindless drones, cells (we are placing an emphasis on nervous cells in this paper) are in fact unique, independent, oftentimes unpredictable entities. Modern*

---

[41] See Edwin W. Taylor, Thomas D. Pollard (Feb 2001) *E.B. Wilson Lecture: The Cell as Molecular Machine* for an example. Retrieved from http://www.ncbi.nlm.nih.gov/pmc/articles/PMC30940/

*evidence in support of this theory can be found in our present understanding of just how varied and complex cellular means of communication are[42], the vast amount of new nervous cell types that are being discovered[43], what influences cellular actions[44], etc. (For more on this, you may visit Jon Lieff's excellent blog on the subject.[45])*

*Cells are much smaller than humans. Cells move much faster than humans as well (again, we are placing an emphasis on nervous cells, which are known to be able to send upwards of a hundred nervous impulses every second) - but that's true only when interpreting things from our human perspective. It doesn't mean that cells are small, or that they move very fast from the perspective of a cell - indeed, given the fact that cellular action & communication have to be very precise despite the microscopic area in which they unfold and their impressive speed by human standards, evidence points to the contrary. There will be more said on the matter of temporal relativity throughout the paper, but for the sake of the argument, entertain this assumption from this point: That a day passing from the perspective of a human being can equal to a year's passing from the perspective of a cell. (Again, emphasis on nervous cells.)"*

---

[42] Jon Lieff (September 21, 2014 )*The Remarkable Language of Cells*. Retrieved from http://jonlieffmd.com/ blog/the-remarkable-language-of-cells

[43] Jon Lieff (October 12, 2014 ) *How Many Different Kinds of Neurons Are There*. Retrieved from http://jonlieffmd.com/blog/how-many-different-kinds-of-neurons-are-there

[44] Jon Lieff (October 19, 2014 ) Does Activity Determine Synaptic Creation and Pruning Retrieved from http://jonlieffmd.com/blog/does-activity-determine-synaptic-creation-and-pruning

[45] http://jonlieffmd.com/

"...Based upon the points made thus far, we may entertain the possibility that **a human's conscious focus is essentially comprised of the elements synthesized by that human's nervous cells and networks of nervous cells that have the necessary qualities to attract their collective attention** (e.g. particular ideas, feelings, sensations, etc.), **and that this conscious focus is not unlike the collective attention of human beings within human society**, which is essentially comprised of elements synthesized by human beings and human networks (e.g. songs, books, movies, videos of cats playing the piano...basically, any element that has its essence in the information it carries, rather than its physical basis) that have the necessary qualities to become very popular within human society. This is the together-knowing theory of consciousness.

Note: 'Collective attention' may sometimes be referred to as 'collective focus' (as in 'collective focus of cells and cellular networks', or 'collective focus of human beings'). The two terms may be used interchangeably."

"...But are we able to offer further evidence in favor of this hypothesis? To address this question, entertain the following thought experiment:

Imagine that a group of very large extraterrestrials (each one roughly the size of Earth), and also very slow (for whom a human year would be the equivalent to the timespan of merely a day) have their spaceship discover a "strange fluorescence" emanating from Earth's surface as they peruse the galaxies. As a consequence, large as they are, they approach the vicinity of Earth, and discover human society growing on it. Also imagine that it's the first time they encounter anything remotely resembling human society in their entire history of space explorations. How would they define human society? From their perspective (so large and so...slow) they would see human society as a whole - as kind of a moss-like organism streaked along Earth's surface (not unlike how a human being sees the human body as a unified whole, even though we know it to be made up of cells.) Despite the fact that they would be looking at human society, these extraterrestrials wouldn't be able to perceive individual humans at first, because for them, human beings would be of a microscopic size.

Let's imagine however that these are science prone lifeforms, so they use microscopes, endoscopes and so on to analyze this "being" growing on Earth's surface down to its "microscopic" structure...and they discover the existence of humans. Following a healthy degree of observation, would they not proclaim us in the end the fundamental structural and functional units of human society, responsible for such things as human society's metabolic function, the growth of its body, etc., just like how we've defined the cell as the fundamental structural and functional unit of the human body? From their perspective, they probably would.

But at the same time, would these humongous and slow aliens not have a very simplistic view of humans, due to extremely limited information they (and their instruments) can pick up from complex human action because of the difference in size and speed between them and us? For example, they wouldn't be able to decode human speech; A person holding a one hour monologue would be compressed in time for the alien scientists to an instant...to a "sound impulse" at most, if their instruments would be equipped with the ability to pick up human speech at all. This is much like how we interpret electrical/electrochemical interactions taking place between nervous cells as "nervous impulses", rather than cellular speech, or anything as complex as that. In other words, the perspective of the alien scientists is becoming very similar to our human perspective of cells."

"...To illustrate the potency of the analogy between *the alien scientists' relationship to a human* and *a human's relationship to a cell*, imagine that the alien scientists decide to send an asteroid towards Earth, though from a safe distance to emulate a natural occurrence, and just stand back to observe the results. And let's say that our astronomers observe it in safe time, and that we eventually decide to send a missile to obliterate the incoming asteroid. Would the alien scientists from their perspective not interpret the sending of the missile as **the action of human society**, rather than the result of countless human beings that were involved in such a defense response? And isn't this much like how we interpret catching a ball during a play of catch as the action of the human being playing, even though we know that the person's body is in fact made up of countless cells, which are acting in concert to catch the ball? It is just natural from the human size and speed to interpret things that way in the latter case, in the same way that it is natural from the size and speed of the alien scientists to interpret the sending of the missile as the action of human society. [46]..."

"...Imagine again how human society looks from the perspective of the alien scientists. See her as an organism growing on the surface of Earth. It would look like an organism, surely, but a multicellular

---

[46] A more in depth account of the alien scientists thought experiment and its many uses, as well an explanation as to why it is such a potent analogy to a human's relationship with a cell can be found in the book *In Principio Res* by Narcis Marincat, from which this paper draws its inspiration.

*organism? No, a multicellular organism is by definition one whose fundamental structural and functional units are cells. Then what type of organism is human society? Well, if a multicellular organism is an organism whose fundamental structural and functional units are cells, then let us define organisms whose fundamental structural and functional units are multicellular organisms as* **multizoa[47] organisms.**

*Let us then look at human society as being a multizoa organism. What can be said about it? Well, the first striking thing that presents itself is that human society is a self-emergent multizoa organism, the first of its kind; It does not have any parent. This is in contrast with any multizoa organism similar to human society that may arise in the future, because it would trace its ancestry to human society. For example, if we were to develop the means for interstellar travel, the colonies we would establish on other planets would, from the perspective of the alien scientists, emerge through a process that can be named multizoa reproduction. And the relationship between human society and any multizoa organism that would descend from it would bear much resemblance to the relationship between the first cell that emerged within nature (dubbed by human scientists as the protocell) and all other cells that descended from it through reproduction; Or the relationship between the first multicellular organism, and all other multicellular organisms that were its descendants.*

*Now, was the very first multicellular organism conscious in the same way that a present-day human is conscious? Of course not. Consciousness evolved over many multicellular generations to get to the level it is today, so we may say that the consciousness of that*

---

[47] Zoia is the greek term for "animals."

*first multicellular organism - if we are to name it consciousness - would have been primitive in comparison to the consciousness of present day human beings. In conclusion, we may extrapolate that the elements which emerge within the collective focus of human beings inhabiting human society today (books, movies, news articles, etc.) are likely primitive in relation the elements that will emerge within the collective focus of human beings inhabiting any multizoa descendant of human society."*

# I. Introduction

As outlined in the preface, the points relevant to our present topic that the first paper has revealed are:

a. that human society is a multizoa organism - that is, an organism whose fundamental structural and functional units are multicellular organisms, in particular human beings, not unlike how the human body is a multicellular organism - that is, an organism whose fundamental structural and functional units are cells, in particular human cells.

b. that human consciousness is essentially comprised of those elements (ideas, feelings, sensations) synthesized by the cells and cellular networks of a human's nervous system upon which those cells and cellular networks focus collectively, which is not unlike how some of the elements synthesized by human beings (books, movies, songs…essentially, any element whose essence lies in the information it carries rather than the medium which holds it) have the necessary qualities to attract the collective attention of human beings within human society and become very popular. This is the together-knowing theory of consciousness.

In other words, you are the consciousness of one organism (your human body) whose thoughts and actions arise from the actions, interactions, choices of its basic units - your cells; While at the same time, you are a basic unit within another organism (human society), with your actions, interactions, contributions, choices giving rise and contributing to the collective focus of human beings (which based on this theory can be considered human society's conscious thoughts) and the projects human beings throughout human society undergo together (from which those projects that have a marked effect outside of human society can be considered human society's conscious actions).

To phrase it more poignantly and also put it in a definitive form:

You are the consciousness of one organism (your human body) whose thoughts and actions arise from the actions, interactions, choices of its basic units - your cells; While at the same time, you are a basic unit within another organism (human society), with your actions, interactions, contributions, choices giving rise and contributing to this organism's conscious thoughts and actions.

Taking this in consideration, it follows that your health, your well-being (both as the consciousness of your body and as the human being as a whole) is intimately connected to the health and well-being of your cells. So then, ask yourself, how would you like for the basic units of your body, your cells, to treat their neighboring cells? Whatever the answer may be, you, as the basic unit of human society, should seek to treat your neighboring human in the same way. For you are to human society what the cells of your body are to you, and if you would like for the cells of your body to, for example, treat their neighboring cells with empathy, to help them flourish and thrive so that you can flourish and thrive, than it follows that one should seek do the same for one's neighbor, so that human society can thrive. In other words, the moral precept that can be extracted from this is **do unto your neighbor as you would have the cells of your body do unto their neighboring cells.**

At the same time, your conscious thoughts are elements synthesized by your cells, just as the elements you synthesize may emerge within the collective focus of human beings (i.e. may become very popular within human society). So, ask yourself, what kind of elements would you like for the cells of your body to synthesize and help elevate within your consciousness? Here too, whatever the answer may be, you, as the basic unit of human society, should treat the collective focus of human beings in the same way, for you are to the collective focus of human beings what the cells of your body are to your consciousness. For example, let us assume that you want for the (nervous) cells of your body to, whenever possible, synthesize and elevate within your consciousness useful, creative thoughts that instill conscious happiness (from simple joke onwards), that generate conscious awe (for example, the feeling of gratitude for simply being alive), that help you establish meaningful goals (e.g. eating right, exercising properly) and that help you achieve the goals in question in a way that's intelligent and empathetic towards your basic units (empathetic in the sense that if you were to get a creative idea about how to achieve the goal you set upon that entails cutting your right arm, you would probably not welcome it). In a word, elements that help make the organism you are a better place for the greatest number of your cells. Based on the together-knowing theory of consciousness, this means that a. such elements are synthesized by the cells of your nervous system, and b. that your cells\cellular networks pass along those elements between them until they emerge within the collective focus\your conscious awareness. So then, you should synthesize and help elevate within the collective focus of human beings elements that generate the collective awe of people, that lead to their happiness, that help people establish meaningful collective goals beneficial to human society as a whole - that is, goals which refer to the general population of human beings and to which the general population would agree to - and elements that help them achieve the goals in question in a way that's intelligent and empathetic towards all the basic units within human society (by passing elements you know of that you consider hold these qualities among the members of your social environment). In a word, elements that have the potential to help make human society a better place for the greatest number of people. (These elements can be of any nature, from books to TV shows, to academic papers, to inventions....Elements that are synthesized or discovered by people around the world.) So, the moral precept that can be extracted from this is to **do unto the collective focus of human beings within human society as you would have the cells of your body do unto the consciousness of your cellular society.**

These then are the two main precepts of this approach to morality: Treat your neighbor as you would have the cells of your body treat their neighboring cells.

and

Do unto the collective focus of human beings within human society as you would have the cells of your body do onto your consciousness.

It is worth noting that one is not compelled to follow these moral guidelines in any way from a spiritual standpoint. They are materialist moral guidelines that arise strictly from the juxtaposition of organisms - that of the human body, and of human society - and the only reason that one should follow them is because they are **logical and useful**, both for the individual self as well as for human society as a whole. In this introduction and the following chapter we are addressing their logical basis.[48] Following that, we'll address their utility.

## II. Counterargument: The Validity Of Conscious Desires

One counterargument that can be brought to these precepts is to say that they are merely based on one's conscious desires for one's basic units. (e.g. you consciously desire your cells to be empathetic towards one another...) and what is to say that your conscious desires bear weight in this case?

But the reason why your conscious desires hold validity for your cells is two fold:

---

[48] For those that are not satisfied with the brief explanation of the logical foothold of these moral precepts, you can find a more detailed, technical explanation at www.inprincipiores.com/wp-content/uploads/2015/A_Novel _Approach_To_Morality_Addendum_-_Logical_Argumentation.pdf
This detailed explanation was initially intended as a chapter of this paper, but was left out in the interest of simplicity and brevity.

First, because you are more "intelligent" than your individual cells, in that your conscious thoughts are the elements that the cells and cellular networks of you body have deemed worthy to bring into their collective focus by assimilating them and passing them throughout their social environment, so they are a careful selection of everything that your cells and cellular networks synthesize, and thus your conscious opinions hold great weight.[49]

And second, because you, as the consciousness of your body, desire what is best for all your cells, both at an individual and at a collective level - both logically, for based on the together-knowing theory of consciousness, that will lead you to thrive. And intuitively, for you will feel good when your cells feel good on a collective level. (e.g. when your cells have to fight an infection for example, you feel sick. When cells throughout your body are thriving and work in harmony, you feel healthy.)

Translated to apply to human society, if this paper (or any other elements that espouses these moral principles) emerges within the collective focus of human beings and gains the general approval of people, the aforementioned moral precepts will have the same qualities in relation to individual human beings.

---

[49] For a more detailed analysis of this aspect of one's consciousness, see In Principio Res Chapter IV #2.

# III. The Utility Of The Aforementioned Moral Precepts

As mentioned before, these moral precepts do not have a metaphysical, but an entirely materialistic fundament. That is to say, they should be pursued because they are **logical and useful.**

In the last two chapters, we've briefly addressed their logical fundament. In this and the following chapters, we will address their utility.

The counterarguments to their utility may be brought especially on an individual level: Some may like to point out that there is a sizeable number of people today which have a very good life (that, of course, extends to their family and loved ones) precisely by not following the moral guidelines described, but on the contrary, by pursuing the ultimate conclusion of moral relativism mentioned in the paper's abstract (by, for example, being greedy and ruthless).

This point has two sides to it:
1. That they choose not to follow these moral guidelines.
2. That they have a good life by not following these moral guidelines.

The first is an aside that I would nevertheless like to address, while the second is directly related to the topic of this chapter.

In regard to number one, I would like to note that seeing human society as an organism, seeing her consciousness as the collective focus of human beings is a perspective of the world that was not available until now, so the fact that some people do not follow these moral guidelines - and more importantly, that some people have pursued human specializations that (by agreeing with the ultimate conclusion of moral relativism) are in contrast with these moral guidelines, with all the habits that they've acquired in the process, is understandable.

At the same time, any human being that has tried to change one's habits knows that it is not easy to achieve, so any mature person of this generation that, following the logic of seeing human society as an organism, seeks to change one's habits in order to agree with the moral conclusions revealed is commendable, rather than those who will still stick to their habits if they are in contrast with these conclusions being damnable. The next generations will have a much easier time of seeing the value of these conclusions objectively, for they may become aware of them before they will have acquired habits that stand in contrast with these moral guidelines.

As to number two - that is, that some people have a good life (which, of course, extends to their family and loved ones) precisely by not pursuing these moral guidelines, this is true only when looking from a very narrow, short-term perspective, that does not take into consideration the fact that:

a. The development of multizoa reproduction, which would improve the quality of life of future human beings markedly, including the descendants of the people in question and their families, would require the cooperation of human beings found throughout human society functioning at their optimum level. (something that these moral precepts recommend we seek to achieve). (Chapter IV & V)

b. Providing human beings found throughout human society with their basic necessities sustainably & unconditionally (a goal that, as we shall prove, naturally arises from following the logical thread of these moral precepts) would increase the probability that elements will be synthesized unpredictably within human society which will have the potential to make the world a better place for all, including for those people that currently have the most power and influence within human society, or those that currently consider themselves better off by not following those moral precepts. (Chapter VI & VII)

# IV. Utility: The Kings Thought Experiment

If you were to have to choose, would you prefer it for your descendants to have lived as kings in 13$^{th}$ century Europe, or as relatively prosperous middle-class people in contemporary society?

And to put this question in perspective, let us take the example of king Edward the First of England - which ruled England in the 13$^{th}$ century - and his family. Living in palaces, enjoying good food, clean water, and an extensive body of servants, king Edward *et al* had a most luxurious lifestyle compared to that of common folk in medieval Europe. However, historical records show that from the 16 children Queen Eleanor bore the king between 1255 and 1284[50], 10 of them died during childhood, with only 6 managing to live beyond age 11. Of those, only three – just 18 per cent – lived beyond the age of forty, despite the royal family having the best doctors of the time at their disposal. That's because medicine was primitive in that period, unable to do much to keep the children of even the most affluent members of society safe. Fast forward to today, and, thanks to contributions brought these past centuries by human beings living throughout human society, many of the

---

[50] Yuval Noah Harari (2014) Sapiens: A Brief History Of Humankind

diseases to which children succumbed in former times are no longer challenging the offspring of the average person in the industrialized world. Moreover, life expectancy has doubled, from mid-thirties to about 64 years worldwide. But medicine was not the only human field that can be considered primitive during that time compared to how it is today. So were the (other) sciences, the arts, technology. The quality of life has improved markedly, with a great many more possibilities in virtually all aspects of human life made generally available to people of all classes. As a consequence, though they were royalty, the quality of life, the scope of their horizon, the possibilities that King Edward *et. al.* had at their disposal as human beings were quite limited compared to those of even the middle-class person in industrialized society living today. Among other things was their degree of understanding the world around them: they had no knowledge of gravity, the composition of stars, atoms, cells, the fundamental laws of nature, etc…One could say that they were ignorant, but, of course, due to of no fault of their own…much of the human contributions that amassed to the present day knowledge of the world which we use to alleviate our ignorance (however slightly) simply weren't there.

So then, applying this question to present-day possibilities, would you like for your descendants to have a lot of power and influence within the organism that we are part of as it is at this stage of development, or would you rather them be "middle-class" in an organism that would be as different from ours as human society in the 13$^{th}$ century was from our present day society? What do you think they would prefer? The answer may very well be the latter, however at this stage in human society's development, in order for the difference between our world and that of our descendants to be the same as the difference between the world of 13th century Europe and that of ours, human beings would have to work together, as one organism. And in particular, because it is only through a massive, large-scale, long-term operation which would include human beings found throughout human society that we would be able to develop human society's ability to reproduce.

# V. Utility: Multizoa Reproduction

The difference between the first cell to have emerged within nature - the protocell - and modern cells like those of the human body is huge - present day cells are much more evolved, more complex, better adapted to their environment, etc. Also, the difference between the first multicellular organism and the modern day human being is no less tremendous - multicellular organisms have evolved a great deal since the initial emergence of multicellular life in all aspects, not just in their conscious abilities.

Now, it has already been mentioned in the former papers and in the preface of the present one that human society is a protomultizoa organism - that is to say, it is the first of its kind, self-emergent, does not have any parent. And if the difference between the first cell to have emerged within nature and all other cells that came after it bear any witness, or for that matter the difference between the first multicellular organism that emerged within nature and all other multicellular organisms that came after it, then our human society is likely very primitive in comparison to its potential multizoa descendants - in other words, the colonies that we would establish on other planets, or the starships that we would build and their successors would come to be much more evolved, likely surpassing human society in virtually every field. And that would mean that the human beings within these multizoa organisms - our descendants - would likely have their horizons much more expanded than ours, as we have our horizons more expanded the inhabitants of 13$^{th}$ century Europe, with a similar wide difference in the quality of life.

Indeed, they would have at their disposal the innovation that our multizoa organism has taken a long time to develop - like ways of harnessing electricity, ships, cars, airplanes, computers, the internet - and they would be able to build upon these developments from their inception. This would include, for example, the possibility to try out new models of organization that take advantage of these technologies without the stigma of having to demolish old ones in the process, but by simply pursuing the natural, playful course laid out by human ingenuity to experiment, and construct anew.

The recognition that our multizoa organism is the first of its kind and therefore likely primitive in comparison to its potential descendants instills a certain degree of humility, but it also points to the incredible, unique position that our human society is in, for we have the possibility to be the very start of a phylogenetic tree that is entirely new in nature's recorded history: A multizoa tree of life that may transform nature in the universe as much as the multicellular tree of life has transformed nature on Earth.

However, in order to take advantage of this opportunity that nature has given us, we, as the basic units of human society, would have to develop the "reproductive systems" of human society in useful time - that is to say, to develop the systems that would give human society the ability of establishing colonies on other planets and\or of constructing starships during its lifetime, a development which would require tremendous cooperation between human beings and human networks throughout our human society. Such cooperation requires a well-organized multizoa organism of sound body[51] and mind[52]. A multizoa organism which helps the basic units throughout its body thrive, so that they can bring contributions that, referring to our present topic, will eventually materialize into the organism's ability to reproduce. If that seems a utopic vision, we shall see in the following chapter how the present day human body does this for its cells all the time, with incredible results.

So, in the end, this seems to be the exam that nature has laid in front of our multizoa organism. Will we, as the basic units of this organism, be able to learn how to cooperate in useful time in order to develop this organism's ability to reproduce? It is a tough exam, but the benefits of passing it are unmeasurable, for if we do, we will become the first member in a multizoa phylogenetic tree that may spread into eternity. (All human disagreements seem to fade in comparison to this goal, do they not?)

However, this task is not one to be tackled with by a few bright minds, but by a lot of bright minds.[53] Or to put it differently, not by a nascent multizoa consciousness, but by a healthy, mature multizoa consciousness, that has gained some experience with how to think up solutions to complex problems and implement them. And in order for such a healthy, mature multizoa consciousness to arise, we would have to start with the basics, and lay the fundamental groundwork onto which it can be constructed.

---

[51] i.e. That is, whose human beings are healthy.

[52] i.e. That is, have the elements which emerge within the collective focus of human beings inhabiting its body be elements that are conducive to their happiness and well-being, both on an individual as well as on a collective level.

[53] For an example of the difficulties encountered in establishing colonies within the solar system alone, see Koki *et. al.* AN INDEPENDENT ASSESSMENT OF THE TECHNICAL FEASIBILITY OF THE MARS ONE MISSION PLAN.

# VI. Providing Human Beings With Their Basic Necessities Unconditionally As A Short-Term Goal

Right know, your body has a nutrient distribution system that is very efficient, which is why you do not have to eat all the time for cells throughout your body to get the glucose that they need, or you don't have to breathe as if you are running a marathon so that cells throughout your body get the oxygen that they require. This nutrient distribution system ensures that the cells all around your body have their basic necessities met as long as those nutrients exist in the body - in other words, as long as you eat and breathe properly. This, among other things, is what allows your cells (including your nervous cells) to do their thing without having to focus a large amount of energy upon satisfying their basic necessities individually.

But imagine for a moment that this nutrient distribution system doesn't exist, or that it is very inefficient, and that as a consequence, the cells within your nervous system would have to ensure their basic necessities individually from their environment in order to survive. It was postulated earlier that the cells of your nervous system synthesize the elements (e.g. ideas, feelings, sensations) which can become part of your conscious awareness. But for them to actually deal with synthesizing these elements, or to turn their attention to the most deserving elements that are made available by their social environment, these cells have to be specialized in the relevant fields.

As an analogy with human society, there is a noteworthy difference between an idea and a feeling - as is the difference between a book and a movie. And in order for a human or a group of people to make a high quality movie, they need to have certain information, certain abilities that differ from those required to make a high quality book for example - abilities that develop in time, with practice. The same goes for nervous cells: They need time and practice to develop abilities which lead to the synthesis of the varied array of elements which emerge within one's consciousness. And one factor that plays a big role in the time-availability necessary to follow these specializations is that these cells have their basic necessities satisfied through the efficient nutrient distribution system mentioned. To put it in human terms, human cells don't have to "worry about" where they get their "bread" tomorrow, and so they are liberated from having to acquire specializations that is linked to that worry, and instead have the freedom to follow specializations like those of nervous cells, which allow them to do things like collectively think about the organism they are part of as a whole. If they would have had to ensure their basic necessities individually, the stem cells that became nervous cells would have acquired other specializations, and would have engaged in other activities that don't have as much to do with the synthesis of thoughts...for they would have perished otherwise. And without cells to engage in such activities, your cognitive capacity would be null, would disappear...the consciousness of your body would cease to exist. In the fortunate case that some sporadic cells would still be able to synthesize relevant elements, your thoughts would be like the flickers of light emitted by a small population of fireflies amidst a large forest. In other words, you would likely have a thought once in a while, and a truly interesting thought probably rarer than that.

Now ask yourself, in this situation, what do you consider those sporadic thoughts which emerge within your consciousness should refer to? Well, seeing as how, in the together-knowing theory of consciousness, your thoughts are elements that your cells\cellular networks focus upon collectively, you would probably consider "valuable thoughts" to be those which seek to find a way of giving cells and cellular networks throughout your body their basic necessities efficiently and sustainably, so that they may have the time and resources to synthesize and help elevate within their collective focus elements that are useful to the organism they are part of as a whole - in other words, so that your consciousness would mature, grow strong.

Now, let us juxtapose this with analysis with current the position of human society. Presently, human beings within human society have to acquire their basic necessities individually, which oftentimes means acquiring whatever specializations are made available to them by their environment, many of which require much time and cognitive resources and are unrelated to the synoptic perspective of human society. As such, to ask people to focus sustainably on human society as a whole, to contribute in unique ways to the collective focus of human beings, to seek to spread the elements that they feel holds promise throughout human society or to help develop the reproductive capabilities of human society seems misplaced for a large population of humans that have more immediate concerns, even more so when we take into account the fact that many people have not just themselves, but a family that they have to look after as well, for whose basic necessities and possibility to thrive they are responsible.

This situation is taking a toll on human society's cognitive abilities, which is why this paper argues that the first step in developing human society's ability to reproduce is to combine human creativity, human ingenuity, human ambition to reach the goal of providing human beings found throughout human society with their basic necessities unconditionally.

On that note, proposing this goal does not mean to say that it should be done in just any way...but to have it accomplished as a well-thought action. There are for example models of autonomous homes, which can offer shelter, electricity, water, sewage and even food without them having to be connected to a centralized grid, with a minimal cost both financially and for the planet. A good example of such homes is the Earthship model, developed by Michael Reynolds and his team. Of course, these types of homes are still at their early stages of development, but the more they would be built, the more they would be improved, be made more efficient, more comfortable, etc. The people that would build them would come up with new ideas, new systems, like it happens in any field. To put it in terms of the together-knowing theory of consciousness, these models of homebuilding would arise within the collective focus of human beings - human society would think of them, and with time, this thinking process would improve them, in the same way that the ideas which arise within your consciousness, when you apply them and then you consider how they turned out, you may improve.

And if these types of homes would be built on a widespread scale, people would always have a basis...they wouldn't have to worry about their basic necessities, they could focus towards other aspects of life. And on this basis, we could build anything else, up until acquiring human society's capacity to reproduce.

Incidentally, the goal of providing human beings throughout human society their basic necessities unconditionally is also in line with the moral code that arises from the juxtaposition of organisms: Do unto your neighbor as you would have the cells of your body do unto their neighboring cells. For if in the scenario in which the nutrient distribution system of your body is lacking, you, as the consciousness of your body, would like for your cells and cellular networks to find a way of efficiently and sustainably provide the basic necessities to their peers so that your conscious thoughts may thrive, then we, as the basic units of human society, should seek to provide the basic necessities to ourselves and our neighbors efficiently and sustainably as well, so that the consciousness of human society may thrive. And as the former case would be in the best interest of your cells, so too can be surmise that the latter would be in the best interest of human beings living throughout human society.

# VII. Utility: Novel Elements That Are Beneficial To All

One of the moral precepts that we've mentioned before was "Do unto the collective focus of human beings as you would have the cells of your body do onto the consciousness of your cellular society." Which means that if you want for the cells of your body to synthesize and help elevate within your conscious awareness elements that, in a word, help make the organism you are a better place for the greatest number of your cells, then so should you seek to aid in the synthesis and in the elevation within the collective focus of human beings elements that, in a word, help make the organism we are all part of a better place for the greatest number of human beings.

What this means is that if these moral precepts are generally adopted, then more elements which have the potential to make the world a better place for the greatest number of human beings will emerge within our collective focus, will become very popular. This is desirable because things that are very popular get funded (oculus rift, the new virtual reality headset that is making waves in the VR industry is a good contemporary example), things that are very popular get disseminated (general example: the widespread distribution of popular movies, books, songs, video games), things that are very popular get adopted (the car), things that are very popular get improved upon (example: the ever-improving novel designs for 3d printers that seek to make them more efficient, simpler, less expensive, etc.), things that are very popular get analyzed, scrutinized (example: the unfortunate case of airplane crashes). Things that are very popular become the inspiration for other elements humans synthesize (example: a popular movie leading to the synthesis of fan art, blog posts, documentaries, spin-offs, etc.). In a word, whatever human society consciously focuses upon, grows. And if what human society will consciously seek to focus upon will be elements that have the potential to make human society a better place for the greatest number of human beings, then that's what will grow through our collective focus. [54]

---

[54] This is not unlike how when you consciously focus upon something, it grows; It grows both informationally within your mind by way of the related elements your nervous cells synthesize that may emerge within your consciousness, and also biophysically, as the nervous cells and cellular networks which played a role in synthesizing your object of focus are allocated with physical resources. (For a more detailed analysis of this topic, see In Principio Res, Chapter IV #5-#9 on Growth.)

What may these elements specifically be? They can be anything from technological innovations, novel scientific theories, or other types of elements that we don't yet know of, but that human creativity makes possible. The main characteristic of these elements is that they have the potential to make the world a better place for a large number of human beings, regardless of social class, race, creed, etc., and that they will attract the collective attention of human beings by virtue of that potential. The answer to this question is a bit like asking yourself what specific solutions will emerge within your consciousness when you start focusing upon a problem you have just encountered. You don't know the answer to the latter question, which is why you are focusing upon finding a solution. What you do know (intuitively) is that a solution is likely to emerge within your consciousness when you focus upon it.

Worth noting is that the area in which those elements that have made the world a better place in the past were synthesized was unpredictable (e.g. the airplane, the computer, the telescope, the word wide web protocols, etc.). What is known however is that in order for the people which synthesized these elements to have done so, they would have had to have their basic necessities met, either because they worked in the field that was related to their endeavors, because they were helped by their families, because their projects were financed by others, etc. We may also postulate the reverse - that those people who did not have their basic necessities met, though they may have had the right inspiration to synthesize such elements, would have not pursued that inspiration due to lack of time\resources. This unfortunate possibility could be eliminated in the future by seeking to provide human beings throughout human society with their basic necessities unconditionally in a way that is sustainable, a goal that has been mentioned in the former chapter.

So, finding a way to provide human beings with their basic necessities is generally desirable not only because it will help to achieve the long-term goal of multizoa reproduction and thus help multizoa organisms evolve, but also because short-term, it will nurture the synthesis and funding of elements that have the potential to help make the world a better place in novel, unpredictable ways for all human beings, regardless of wealth, social status, race, creed, etc., including the people living within human society who some believe are in fact better off precisely by not following these moral precepts.

## VIII. The Aforementioned Moral Precepts In Contemporary Society

What would be some of the effects of these moral precepts in today's society should they be applied? There would be quite a few, but we will enumerate a couple of them:

First, there are certain cells within the human body that have more power and influence than any other, like the insulin-producing cells in the pancreas, the endocrine cells of the thyroid gland, or the dopamine-producing cells found in the part of the brain called the substantia nigra. When these cells do not perform their task properly, diseases on the level of the entire human body can appear, including acromegaly, diabetes, Parkinson's, etc. Knowing this, one, as the consciousness of one's body, would likely want for these cells to do the task that they've been assigned, so that one's body is healthy and one's consciousness can focus on other matters than finding solutions to health issues.

At the same time, there are certain human beings within human society that have more power and influence than most people (whether acquired, inherited, etc.) such as those human beings that have a lot of wealth, political figures, etc. And when these people do not use that wealth or influence properly, human society can experience phenomena that may be considered multizoa diseases (example: the dot-com crash, housing bubble, economic depression, etc.)

The moral precepts described here say that if the consciousness of these people would like for the cells of their respective bodies to use their position to the benefit of the general population of their neighboring cells, then they should do the same within human society - that is, they should use their position to the benefit of the general population of human beings - because the two precepts are equivalent.

Second, on a simpler note, how would you like for your cells to treat their neighboring cells? Well, essentially, you may want for cells to help one another be at their optimum efficiency. If one cell is sick or injured, you would like for its neighboring cells to, whenever possible, help heal it. If one cell is ailing, you would like for its neighboring cells to, whenever possible, discover the cause and help mend it. Why? Because you, as the consciousness of your cellular society, arise from the interactions taking place between cells found throughout your body, and if they function at their optimum level, "you" function at your optimum level.

So then, based on the moral precepts outlined, one should seek to, whenever possible, help one's neighbors be at their optimum level. If one neighbor is sick or injured, one should seek to, whenever possible, help heal him or her. If one human is ailing, one should seek to discover the root cause and help mend it.

In summary, these moral precepts promote kindness and compassion towards one's neighbor whatever one's position within human society is.

# IX. Summary: Moral Precepts Based On Present Knowledge Of The World That Are Logical And Useful

So, by looking at the relation between one's role within the human body and one's role within human society, the following moral precepts have come to light:

Do unto your neighbor as you would have the cells of your body do unto their neighboring cells.

and

Do unto the collective focus of human beings as you would have the cells of your body do unto the consciousness of your cellular society.

These moral precepts are not only logical (Chapter I-II), but also useful.

Useful short-term, because they will lead to the synthesis and nurturing of elements that have the potential to make the world a better place for the greatest number of human beings, regardless of social class, creed, race, etc. (Chapter VII).

Useful long-term, because by following their natural conclusion to provide human beings throughout human society with their basic necessities (Chapter VI), it will help lay the groundwork for developing human society's ability to reproduce as a multizoa organism (Chapter V). Based on the juxtaposition of organisms, multizoa reproduction will ultimately provide future generations of human beings with an exponential increase in possibilities, knowledge about the world and well-being, as the difference between our society and the societies they will be living in will be much like the difference between the more primitive first generation of multicellular organisms to have evolved within nature and later ones.

On a more individual note, the moral precepts outlined promote kindness, encouraging one to, whenever possible, help one's fellow human beings thrive no matter their role within human society, as one would like for the cells of one's body help their neighboring cells thrive (Chapter VIII).

# IS HUMAN SOCIETY A MULTIZOA ORGANISM?

What is human society in the overall biological hierarchy of nature? This paper argues that human society is a multizoa organism - that is, an organism comprised of many animals - just like multicellular organisms are organisms comprised of many cells. Evidence for this theory will be provided, counterarguments addressed, and then we will briefly outline the theory's utility.

## I. Introduction

In order to acquire an objective perspective of human society, let us introduce a thought experiment.

Imagine that a group of extraterrestrials peruse the galaxies on a trip of exploration, when, upon venturing close to our solar system, their spaceship picks up a strange fluorescence emanating from the surface of our planet, so they decide to take a closer look and investigate. Now, these are not your average extraterrestrial beings - they are extremely large. So large, in fact, that each one of them is comparable in size to our planet. Not only that, but imagine that with this size difference there would be a difference in their speed, such that a year from our human perspective would equal for them to the timespan of merely a day. Finally, these extraterrestrials reach the vicinity of Earth, they take their endoscope-like instruments, peer through Earth's cloudy atmosphere, and what do they see? Well, they see that an organism is growing on the surface of this planet, and rather than being "fluorescence", what their spaceship picked up was in fact a type of bioluminescence emanating by this organism. This organism would of course be human society. Here it's important to note that these extraterrestrials would be completely different in nature from us, and that this is the first time they would see anything like this organism in their entire history of space explorations.

Now, put yourself in the extraterrestrial's shoes: How would they see human society? Well, they would see it as a whole, as kind of like a slime-mold, a fungus streaked along the Earth's surface. Even if they would be looking at human society, they wouldn't be able to see individual humans, because for them, humans are of a microscopic size. Also, while from our human perspective it is customary to think of human society as apart from nature by, for example, considering man-made buildings or vehicles "artificial", the extraterrestrials wouldn't see any difference from something manmade, and nature made - from their objective perspective, everything from the amazon forest to a busy human metropolis would be nature.

Ok, so they wouldn't be able to see individual humans to the difference in size, but let's say that aliens are science-prone lifeforms, so what they do next is use microscope-like instruments to uninvasively analyze the microscopic structure of this organism growing on the surface of Earth, and in doing so they not only discover the existence of humans, but what they come to conclude based on their findings is that humans are the fundamental structural and functional units of this organism, which are responsible for everything from the metabolic function of this organism (the energy consumed) to its growth (when human beings grow in number, the size of the organism grows). In short, this organism growing on the surface of Earth is made of humans. This is not unlike the perspective of human beings in relation to their fellow man. When one looks at another person, one perceives that person as a whole, as a unified entity even though one knows that the human body one is looking at is in fact made up of countless cells, all acting in cooperation with one another to move the body, to generate thoughts, etc.

At the same time however, the alien scientists would have a very simplistic view of humans, based on the limited information their scientific instruments can pick up from human activity. For example, human speech is a form of communication that is unique to our order of magnitude - just think of how strange it would seem for the alien scientists that we are able to communicate by passing airwaves of various frequencies between one another. In space, there wouldn't be any air, so for them that would be an entirely novel phenomenon. This means that their scientific instruments would probably not be equipped with a microphone that would pick up these airwaves, because they would have no concept of microphones - but even if they would be, due to the difference in speed between us and them, human speech would unfold much too fast for it to be understood by the aliens. For example, an entire human monologue would vanish in the flash of an instant, so they would probably interpret it as a blip, an impulse, and not see it speech for the complex art that it is. No, what they would be able to do though is make assumptions about human beings based on the big picture: For example, they may reach the conclusion that after birth, a human being picks up the general activities of those within its surroundings, because their microscopes would at least allow them to see that if a human was born in an area of human society in which most people can drive cars, that human would also have a high probability of driving a car. Or if a human was born in an area of human society in which most people get their food from big nourishment hubs - supermarkets - that human would also have a high probability of doing the same.

So, bottom line, due to the difference in size and speed between us and them, as well as the limitations of their scientific instruments the alien scientists would have a very simplistic view of humans, and it would just be natural for them to see human society as a whole, and interpret things as such, just like it is natural for human beings to see the human body as a whole, and interpret things as such.

Alright, we can agree that when human society is looked at from the perspective of the alien scientists, it is naturally perceived as an organism. But is it a multicellular organism? No, a multicellular organism is by definition one whose fundamental structural and functional units are cells. Then what type of organism is human society? Well, if a multi*cellular* organism is an organism whose fundamental structural and functional units are cells, then let us define organisms whose fundamental structural and functional units are multicellular organisms as multizoa[55] organisms.

---

[55] Zoia is the greek term for "animals."

# II. Counterargument: An Organism's Actions

One may argue that it is debatable whether or not human society is really an organism, because a proper organism doesn't just look like a single entity, but is also able to act like a single entity.

To address this point, imagine that one of the more adventurous alien scientists sets up an experiment in which he plans to an asteroid like projectile towards Earth and stand back to observe and record the results. The maverick's reasoning is that planets get bombarded by meteorites and asteroids all the time, and that there's no way that the organism they have before them could have grown to the extent that it has without having some sort of defense mechanism in place against such common threats. So, he concludes, sending a projectile that imitated such space objects towards Earth would not only not harm the organism growing on its surface, but would in fact offer the alien scientists the chance to gain a better understanding of it.

As a consequence, let's say that the alien scientists send the projectile from a distance that gives it roughly a human year to reach Earth - which means roughly a day to them - so as to make sure that it simulates a natural occurrence, and that our astronomers notice the incoming asteroid not long after it is sent. That would give human society some time to come with a defense strategy. In the end, a missile is sent from the surface of Earth that eventually reaches the asteroid and obliterates it. From our perspective, we would know that it took a large amount of human cooperation to actually produce this success - from the astronomers that first noticed the incoming asteroid, to the engineers that designed the missile, to the person who ultimately pushed the button to send the missile on its way. But from the perspective of the alien scientists, for whom humans are of a microscopic size and move very fast, the sending of the missile would be seen as the action of human society, rather than the cumulative actions of so many people throughout human society - it would just be natural for them to interpret things that way, just as it is natural for a person to interpret the movements of another human being as that human's actions, rather than the cumulative actions of a large number of cells within that human's body.

Alright, now let's take the experiment one step further. Let's assume that the alien scientists would be so pleased with human society's response, and would gain so much trust in its defense systems that they would agree to send a string of asteroids towards Earth - one each consecutive day from their perspective, so one each consecutive year from ours - to see what happens. What would be the result? Well, assuming for the sake of simplicity that the status quo is kept, as the second asteroid approaches Earth, the people who handled the first defense response would be better able to handle the tasks that they've assumed because they've practiced it before - from the astronomers who would know who to call, to the engineers who would have the plans for the missile, to the people who handled the logistics of it all. So, from the perspective of the alien scientists, what this would translate into is a more timely, perhaps more efficient defense response from the part of human society - a clear indication towards the organism's ability to adapt to its environment, to learn.

# III. Counterargument: An Organism's Evolutionary Tree

One may argue that the concept of multizoa organisms is not really a valid one, not like the concept of multicellular organisms, because multicellular organisms can be classified into taxonomic groups such as species, phyla - in other words, into an evolutionary tree of life - whereas human society is the only multizoa organism that we know of.

To address this argument, imagine that, after performing a number of scientific experiments on our human society, the alien scientists eventually left this galactic area satisfied with the data they've collected. Their species did not come back to our corner of the universe for a few billion years, after which time they remembered human society and decided to see what changed since their kind first ventured here. When they arrived however, what they discovered was quite unexpected: The long-past first expedition that their ancestors went on years ago (billions of years from the perspective of human beings) documented the existence of only one multizoa organism, our human society. But now, upon returning, they were surprised to witness the existence of a large number and variety of multizoa organisms, displaying strikingly different structural differences and behaviors between them. Some of these multizoa organisms were indeed rooted to the surface of planets and somewhat resembled the description of our human society, whereas others had motile, agile bodies and engaged in complex activities - what we would consider to be human-built starships. With the help of their advanced scientific instruments, the alien scientists discovered stationary as well as motile multizoa organisms that lived underwater on various planets as well.

In other words, in contrast to the first expedition, what they now found was an incredible display of multizoa life, with multizoa organisms of various shapes and sizes, adapted to various environments.

Now, they may very well wonder where all this multizoa life came from - Whether multizoa organisms emerge through spontaneous generation, or whether they emerge through reproduction from other multizoa organisms; They may also wonder what mechanisms underlie the capacity of multizoa organisms to diversify, to acquire different traits. And if they were to engage in thorough scientific investigations, they would find that all multizoa organisms emerge through reproduction from other multizoa organisms (That is, a human colony doesn't just appear out of thin air; It can only be established by another human colony, or starship) ; They would probably find fossilized multizoa organisms as well in some parts of the galactic area inhabited by multizoa organisms; They would find that the fossilized and living multizoa organisms fall into a natural order based on the traits that they share, and so they might come up with the concept of a multizoa tree of life (phylogenetic tree). All of this would lead them to consider that multizoa organisms have evolved over time, through generations after generations of multizoa organisms, and that it's probable that at the base of this multizoa tree of life would be a first multizoa organism to have emerged within nature, from which all other multizoa organisms stem. A self-emergent multizoa organism, the first of its kind, quite probably an unlikely event within nature.

What they probably wouldn't know is that this first multizoa organism to have emerged within nature would have been our human society.

That is, really, the first striking conclusion that presents itself when looking at human society as being a multizoa organism: our human society is a self-emergent multizoa organism, the first of its kind; It does not have any parent. This is in contrast with any multizoa organism similar to human society that may arise in the future, because any such multizoa organism would trace its ancestry to our human society. For example, if we were to develop the means for interstellar travel, the colonies we would establish on other planets, the starships that we would build and so on would, from the perspective of the alien scientists, emerge through a process that can be named multizoa reproduction. And the relationship between human society and any multizoa organism that would descend from it would bear much resemblance to the relationship between the first cell that emerged within nature (dubbed by human scientists as the protocell) and all other cells that descended from it through reproduction; Or the relationship between the first multicellular organism, and all other multicellular organisms that were its descendants.

So, the reason that unlike multicellular organisms, there is currently only one multizoa organisms, the reason there are no multizoa species, is because human society is a protoorganism, on par with the protocell and the protomulticellular organism from this standpoint. If human society were to develop its ability to reproduce - that is, to develop the ability to establish colonies on other planets and\or build starships - this would swiftly change.

# IV. Further Evidence: An Organism's Thoughts

Is there more evidence in support of the theory that human society is an organism? One of the features of more evolved organisms is the sense of self. Of course, that requires thinking, which may initially seem inapplicable to human society. But the together-knowing theory of consciousness defines the consciousness of an organism as being comprised of the information-based elements that the organism's fundamental structural and functional units and the networks that they form synthesize (make) which become very popular within that organism.[56] So, a human being's consciousness is comprised of the thoughts, feelings, sensations, mental imagery that his cells synthesize which they focus upon collectively, i.e. that become very popular within the nervous system of that human being; In the same vain, human society's consciousness may be thought of as being comprised of books, movies, songs, news articles, etc. that become very popular within human society, i.e. that attract the collective attention of human beings. This theory of consciousness does not discriminate between multicellular and multizoa organisms.

In this theory of consciousness, an important part of a human's conscious sense of self is the elements her cells and cellular networks synthesize that refer to herself with the first person

---

[56] See Narcis Marincat (2015) CAN CONSCIOUS THOUGHTS BE CONSIDERED "WORKS OF ART" CREATED BY CELLS, MUCH LIKE HOW MOVIES, BOOKS, VIDEO GAMES ARE WORKS OF ART CREATED BY PEOPLE? for a thorough treatment of the subject.

pronoun: I, me, mine, that give off that sense. So, when a person says "I am going to the car", the nervous cells within that person's body synthesized elements that refer to the entire 50 trillion cell population within that body as a single entity.

In contrast, the elements synthesized by humans (books, movies, songs, etc.) that become very popular usually refer to human society using $3^{rd}$ person appellatives, singular and plural, when they do so at all (e.g. human society, all human beings throughout the world), or perhaps with the $1^{st}$ person plural (all of us throughout the world). But imagine what would happen if human beings everywhere would agree to refer to human society with a $1^{st}$ person pronoun that can only refer to human society.

Let us name that $1^{st}$ person pronoun -I-. So, for example, instead of saying "this is human society", we can say "-I- am human society". -I- am human society, the being whose fundamental structural and functional units are human beings living on Earth, in the same way that you are a human, a being whose fundamental structural and functional units are the cells of your body. -I- am human society as a whole, in the same way that you are your body as a whole.[57]

Now, some may argue that such a concept would not be of much use, because everyone would be able to use it to speak in the name of human society as a whole (including writing books/making movies/singing songs that refer to human society in this first-person manner), and thus it is likely that a lot of conflicting ideas, many of

---

[57] The notation of the concept is as follows: The first-person pronoun is accompanied by a dash on each of its sides, and the first letter of the pronoun is capital. So, the pronouns representing human society are "-I-", "-Me-", "-Mine-", etc.

which would not be in concert with what human beings truly believe on a general basis, would be formulated using this concept.

But in the together-knowing theory of consciousness, only the elements synthesized by human beings (e.g. books, movies, songs, blog posts, etc.) that we make very popular through what we, the general population, decide to read\watch\listen to and to share with others would be considered human society's "conscious thoughts" - in other words, only those elements which refer to human society as -I- that human beings throughout human society assimilate and pass among their social environment emerge within human society's consciousness, whether they are in essence books, movies, documentaries, articles, papers, songs, etc. All other such elements that do not have the necessary qualities to attract the collective attention of human beings would remain part of human society's subconscious (for example, a documentary that was not that good, and therefore not that popular) - so in fact, there would be a filter that selects which elements that refer to -Me- would emerge within -My- consciousness.

In that case, through the concept of -I-, the collective focus of human beings would have a separate life, a separate identity from the individual human beings which contribute to and whose attention make up that collective focus. This is not unlike how I, my consciousness is independent from the basic units of my body, that is from the individual cells that make up my body's nervous system, even though it is clear that these cells give rise to my consciousness and my own sense of self.

So, if this language is adopted, the concept of -I- would give human society a self-identity that is independent from individual human beings. What would be the outcome? Would there appear a sense of a multizoa inner monologue within human society that would seek consistency? Would certain elements synthesized by -My- human beings that refer to -Me- remain within -My- subconscious\be filtered out of -My- consciousness because they are not consistent with that inner monologue at a given point in time? We will leave these questions open for future generations of human beings and of multizoa organisms.

What is clear based on this chapter is that with a little widespread human agreement, human society, through the collective focus of human beings, can acquire a sense of self-identity, another line of evidence that validates human society's position as an organism.

# V. Conclusion

In summary, what this paper shows it that human society can be considered a multizoa organism, meaning an organism whose fundamental units are animals, in particular human beings. Evidence stems from areas as diverse as the alien scientists thought experiment (chapter I & II); the concept of multizoa evolution (chapter III); and the study of consciousness (chapter IV).

But is seeing human society as an organism useful in any way? Well, one may conclude that this perspective is useful for human society as a whole in much the same way that a person's conscious perspective of himself as a single entity is useful - in the latter case, it allows one to consider what one is capable of as an organism; It also allows one to asses one's relationship to one's surroundings and the world at large. It allows one to consider one's relationship with other people. And so too is it true in relation to human society. Seeing -Myself- as an organism allows -Me- to consider -My- capabilities when human beings throughout -My- Body work together for common goals. It allows -Me- to see -My- position in the universe in the objective light of biological development. It allows -Me- to consider -My- relationship to any multizoa organisms that -I- may meet, that may arise through reproduction from -Me-, human society.

# Contents

Introduction ........................................................................... 1
Part 1: Explanation ................................................................ 3
   Chapter I. Cells ................................................................... 3
   Chapter II. Consciousness ................................................. 8
   Chapter III. Morality ......................................................... 14
   Chapter IV. Evolution ...................................................... 19
   Chapter V. The Utility Of Moral Precepts ..................... 26
   Chapter VI. Counterarguments ..................................... 36
   Chapter VII. Conclusion .................................................. 44
Part 2: Papers ...................................................................... 48
   Author's Note .................................................................. 48

**CAN CONSCIOUS THOUGHTS BE CONSIDERED "WORKS OF ART" CREATED BY CELLS, MUCH LIKE HOW MOVIES, BOOKS, VIDEO GAMES ARE WORKS OF ART CREATED BY PEOPLE?** ................. 50
   I. Introduction ................................................................. 51
   II. The Collective Focus Effect ....................................... 53
   III. Time's Passing ........................................................... 56
   IV. Thought Experiment: The Alien Scientists ............ 56
   V. The Potency Of The Analogy ..................................... 60
   VI. The Homunculus Fallacy .......................................... 61
   VII. Addressing The Fundamental Differences Between One's Conscious Thoughts And Elements Synthesized By Human Beings ................................................................. 63
   VIII. Conclusion: How Real-Time Conscious Processes Are Explained ........................................................................... 67
   IX. Conclusion: How The Gap Between Cellular Activity And Consciousness Is Bridged ............................................. 69

**CAN THE NOVEL BIOLOGICAL TRAITS OF MULTICELLULAR ORGANISMS BE CONSIDERED CELLULAR INVENTIONS, MUCH LIKE HOW THE STEAM ENGINE, THE CAR, THE ASTRONOMICAL OBSERVATORY ARE HUMAN INVENTIONS?** ............... 71

   Preface ............................................................................. 72

   I. Introduction ................................................................. 79

   II. Speculations, Gathering Evidence And The Final Theory .... 81

   III. Evolution Through The Natural Selection Of Multizoa Organisms That Underwent Random Mutations ................. 85

   IV. Juxtaposition Of Theories .......................................... 86

   V. Counterarguments: The Unpredictable Outcome Of Sexual Reproduction ................................................................. 93

   VI. The Cambrian Explosion Explained ............................ 96

   VII. Conclusion - The Evolution Of Organisms Through The Natural Selection Of Individuals That Underwent Favorable Teleological Mutations ................................................... 100

**A NOVEL APPROACH TO MORALITY: DO UNTO YOUR NEIGHBOR AS YOU WOULD HAVE THE CELLS OF YOUR BODY DO UNTO THEIR NEIGHBORING CELLS** ........................................................... 103

   Preface ........................................................................... 104

   I. Introduction ............................................................... 110

   II. Counterargument: The Validity Of Conscious Desires ...... 114

   III. The Utility Of The Aforementioned Moral Precepts ........ 116

   IV. Utility: The Kings Thought Experiment ....................... 118

   V. Utility: Multizoa Reproduction .................................... 120

   VI. Providing Human Beings With Their Basic Necessities Unconditionally As A Short-Term Goal ............................. 123

   VII. Utility: Novel Elements That Are Beneficial To All .......... 127

   VIII. The Aforementioned Moral Precepts In Contemporary Society ........................................................................... 130

    IX. Summary: Moral Precepts Based On Present Knowledge Of The World That Are Logical And Useful .................................. 132

**IS HUMAN SOCIETY A MULTIZOA ORGANISM?** ....................... 134

    I. Introduction ....................................................................... 134

    II. Counterargument: An Organism's Actions ........................ 138

    III. Counterargument: An Organism's Evolutionary Tree ...... 140

    IV. Further Evidence: An Organism's Thoughts ..................... 143

    V. Conclusion ......................................................................... 146

www.ingramcontent.com/pod-product-compliance
Lightning Source LLC
Chambersburg PA
CBHW071509040426
42444CB00008B/1563